PREFACE

by H. Allen Smith

ON SOUTH LEE STREET in Alexandria, Virginia, stands a trim two-story house with outer walls that are convex—bulging from an accumulation of source material relating to baseball. The master of these premises is Ira L. Smith, a tall, dark, nervously eager man with extraordinary wells of energy inside of him. He is one of those happy humans who make an avocation out of research work. He glories in it.

Since the early 1920s Ira has been haunting the Library of Congress across the river in Washington. He has been in editorial work of one kind and another all his adult life, and this work has usually involved research; but the pleasure he derives from exploring the past has kept him digging and delving far beyond the ordinary requirements of the job at hand. For a good many years he has been spending all his spare hours deep in the bowels of the government's huge library, patiently mining for baseball lore.

7

Ira settled on baseball as an extramural research project for the simple reason that he has baseball in his blood. As a boy in Pueblo, Colorado, he was mascot for the local Western League club. Later, in Denver, he became a semi-pro player of considerable talent. Then along came World War I. As a soldier, Ira was so banged up that he had to abandon all thought of ever continuing as a ball player. Never once, however, has he faltered in his devotion to the game.

When he gets to talking about either baseball or the Library of Congress he turns into a windmill wired for sound, and the rest of the company might as well shut up.

He has become almost a fixture around the Library of Congress. He works usually on Deck B—a locality that is well named, for it resembles a cranny somewhere in the remote interior of a battleship; and he works with photographic equipment, having long ago perfected his own apparatus for copying ancient newspaper stories and magazine articles. There on Deck B he has been flanked by a variety of other researchers. At a table on his right, most recently, has labored a nun engaged upon a broad research project involving one of the saints; and on his left, an elderly woman who has been digging into the history of cats with the intention of someday producing a book to end all books about cats. Sometimes I catch myself visualizing this scene—the three patient scholars at work—and a moment arrives when each of the three comes upon a nugget of information and exclaims over it. From the nun a soft cry of "Bless us!" From the elderly lady a sharper exclamation, "Meeeeow!" And from the man in the middle an eager shout, "Yer out!"

One day last year Ira Smith sat down and took stock of himself and his labors. Here he had this enormous accumulation of baseball material. What was he ever going to do with it? There had always, of course, been a vague idea in his mind that a history of baseball might result from his researches, but he had

8

kept himself so occupied with the actual digging that the thought of publication was quite secondary.

He got to talking about it one day with his friend, Jay Carmody, Washington drama columnist and former sports writer. Jay Carmody spoke to a couple of New York newspapermen about Ira's work, and in the end a sampling of the material he had gathered found its way into the hands of the writer.

This book is the result. It contains no more than a loud hint of the baseball material that is bulging the walls of that house on South Lee Street. Out of Ira's accumulation has come, this time, not a history of baseball. I plunged into it seeking anecdotes and oddities. When I had found enough of them to make a book, I quit. My own job, then, has been one of selecting the stories that interested me most and then putting them on paper, with Ira standing at my elbow to see that I stayed honest and didn't warp or distort his material.

It needs to be explained that Ira's researches cover publications dating from 1860 down to the beginning of World War I. Therein, I think, lies much of the appeal of this present book. These stories are, for the most part, so old that they are almost bound to be "new" to the baseball fans of our day.

Ira has, in passing, accumulated hundreds of first-rate anecdotes that have come out of baseball in more recent years. Many of these, I feel sure, would be brand-new to the reader, yet we decided against using them. By drawing a definite line, by limiting ourselves to stories that appeared in print prior to 1918, we felt that we would be giving the customers a product that was not, paradoxically, second-hand.

Quite understandably, Ira wants to express his gratitude to members of the Library of Congress staff who have been helpful to him. Among them he makes special mention of Henry S. Parsons, now retired, who long was chief of the periodical division; David C. Mearns, director of the reference department;

9

Robert C. Gooch, chief of the general reference and bibliography division; Willard Webb, chief of the stack and reader division; David J. H. Cole, reference assistant; and Chester Atkinson, who is a sort of officer-of-the-day on Deck B.

There will, no doubt, be readers of this book who will remember baseball stories as good or better than those which we have assembled—stories which probably never have found their way into print. If the urge comes upon them to write those stories down, Ira will be glad to get them. After checking them to hell and gone for accuracy, he will add them to his files and eventually his house will bust wide open and fall into the street.

In parting, let me add that I am a fair-to-middling baseball fan, so it goes without saying that my own part in the production of this book has been fun. I will be happy in the thought that you, the reader, may get an equal amount of pleasure from it.

A REMARKABLE baseball game in which nobody pitched attracted a large crowd on June 10, 1897, at Princeton University.

Many professors were present, as was Mrs. Grover Cleveland, and the most excited person in the assemblage was Professor C. H. Hinton, an instructor in mathematics at the university. Professor Hinton was inventor of the pitching machine which occupied the mound that day.

The Hinton Mechanical Pitcher was a sort of baseball gun. It pitched for both sides—the Ivy Club and the team representing the Tiger Inn. Like many human counterparts, the pitching machine took its sweet time between throws so that the game ended after three full innings of play. The box score showed the machine's record for the three innings as follows:

"Strike-outs, 8; Bases On Balls, 1; Wild Pitch, 1; Hits Off Of, 4."

A press dispatch from the field gives us some of the details.

"The gun," it said, "is discharged by the batsman who, when ready for the ball to be delivered, steps upon an electrical intercepting plate which is connected by wires with the trigger of the cannon.

"The speed with which the ball is thrown is regulated by compressed air. Pronglike projectors from the cannon's mouth impart a rotary motion to the sphere when it is discharged, producing a curve in any direction according as the position of the projecting prongs is changed.

"There is but one serious defect in the operation of the machine and that is the long time required for reloading. The frequent delays did not allow a full nine-inning game to be played.

"During the first inning, the batsmen were timid about standing near the plate and the big curves caused them to jump back. But, as the big gun continued to throw strikes, they plucked up courage, stood closer to the plate, and succeeded occasionally in making safe hits."

What happened to the pitching machine after that tryout is not known to your deponents. Perhaps Professor Hinton got discouraged trying to improve it—trying to teach it, say, to chew tobacco. It may even be that the machine still exists and, somewhere in our land, is happily engaged in running a poolroom.

 THE OLDTOWN TEAM of the Northern Maine League was playing at Millinocket one August afternoon in 1902 when Horace Newenham executed his fielding play which places him on the roll of baseball immortals—at least in Maine. Our account of Horace's feat comes from the Portland *Press*.

The Millinocket River flowed past the ball field where the

game was being played. Horace Newenham was playing right field when Barrington, the heaviest hitter on the Millinocket team, belted a terrific drive. Horace was outward bound with the crack of the bat and heard the crowd roar as the ball came out of the clouds and went kerplosh into the middle of the river.

Barrington, the hitter, also saw where his long hit had gone and took his time on the base paths.

Meanwhile Horace arrived at the riverbank. Seeing the ball drifting on the surface in midstream, Horace didn't hesitate. He leaped into the water, swam out, seized the ball, and—the Portland newspaper says he did this—*put it in his mouth.*

Barrington had slowed to a walk by this time, feeling quite pleased with himself, and was on his way from second to third when Horace emerged from the water, snatched the ball out of his own teeth, and heaved it hard. It was a fine throw, and arrived in the hands of the third baseman just ahead of the ambling Barrington, who was promptly tagged out.

IT CAN GET mighty hot in Minnesota in the summertime, and it was hot that fourteenth of July in 1903 when two teams, representing the towns of Benson and Willmar, tangled in a double-header.

All the players were frazzled by the time the second game began, and when that game went into extra innings they were pooped beyond description.

Thielman, the star pitcher for Willmar, dragged himself up to the plate at the opening of the tenth inning. He swung listlessly at a pitch and got a single. The next batter, O'Toole, met the ball solidly and sent it streaking toward the outfield.

Pitcher Thielman, in spite of his vast weariness, started his

13

sprint around the base paths ahead of O'Toole. Midway between second and third Thielman began to slow down and then to stagger. Reaching third, he collapsed in a heap on top of the bag.

Down came O'Toole from second to find Thielman draped over the bag. O'Toole looked toward the outfield and saw that the ball had not yet been retrieved. He knew the rules. It would be illegal for him to pass a runner. So he picked up the pitcher, hoisted his limp body to his shoulder, and hobbled down the line. Reaching home, he lowered Thielman so that one foot dragged across the plate. Then he himself touched it, just a moment before the ball reached the catcher.

Having effected the scoring of two runs, O'Toole lowered Thielman to the ground and players gathered around. A doctor came out of the stands and bent over the pitcher. Finally he straightened up.

"This man," he said, "died back there on third base. His heart broke down under the strain."

Thus a run was scored by a dead man, and if ever an incident in baseball could be labeled "unique," this one would appear to qualify. Yet the old files show that it happened another time, up in New Brunswick, when the Chatham Stars were playing the University of St. Joseph. This time a man named O'Hara collapsed on third base after a teammate got a long hit, and the teammate carried O'Hara's body to the plate just as O'Toole had done with Thielman.

THE CURSE of an infielder's existence is the ball that takes a bad bounce. There have been occasions, of course, where the ball has hit a

pebble or some other object and taken an erratic course favorable to the infielder. Such a "good bounce" came the way of First Baseman William Griffiths back in 1905 at Salt Lake City. That ball, in fact, came real close to offsetting all the bad bounces of baseball history.

Griffiths was in the field for a team called the Rhyolites. A batter for the opposition Beattys sent a ground ball toward first. The ball struck a small stone and shot off at an angle, but landed in the first baseman's glove. He beat the runner to first base easily.

The little stone had given Griffiths a lucky break, but he decided it had no business on the playing field, so he walked over and picked it up. He started to raise his hand to throw it off the field when something caught his eye. He took a careful look at the stone and recognized free gold in it. Then he quietly slipped it into his pocket and went on with the game.

That evening he returned to the ball park with a lantern and spent an hour scratching around in the soil until he had accumulated a bucketful of rocks. By morning he knew that those rocks assayed more than nine hundred dollars to the ton. He called in two friends and with them quietly bought the ball park.

The mine was called First Base and the first shaft entered paying ore at a depth of thirty-three feet. And Infielder Griffiths soon found himself a very wealthy man.

A FOUR-LEGGED SKUNK was the deciding factor in a baseball game at the Patoka park near Hazelton, Indiana, back in 1908. The Patoka ten (nine men and the skunk) defeated the Evansville Sealbacks 7 to 6.

Evansville was ahead when the game reached the sixth inning, at which point one of the Patoka lads slammed the ball to deep right field. The Evansville outfielder saw the fly heading into a cornfield and went charging after it. He disappeared into the cornstalks at a rapid rate and he came out at a rapider one. As he emerged it was seen that he was holding the ball, delicately, as far from his body as he could get it, and with his other hand he was holding his nose. The fly ball had hit a skunk, and the skunk struck back with his chief weapon, which is not his mouth.

During the remainder of the game the wind blew across the diamond from the direction of the cornfield. The Hazelton players apparently were accustomed to such conditions, but not the men from Evansville. Three of the Evansville players became sick, enabling Patoka to come from behind and win the game.

PRESIDENT CHRIS VON DER AHE of the St. Louis Browns surprised members of his team when, at the beginning of the 1894 season, he presented each of them with a new suit of clothes. The fact that all of the suits were identical and were exact duplicates of the suit Chris himself wore made no impression at the moment.

A few weeks later the players found out why their president had been so generous. The boys had been a little lax about training rules, and Chris had figured out a way to trap them. He called in a private detective and told him to hang around certain saloons and watch for customers who were wearing suits "just like the one I got on."

The detective did his duty and turned in a report, and three players were summoned to the president's office. There they were confronted with the evidence, told how they had been trapped, and fined $25 each. One of the three refused to take the punishment meekly.

"Boss," he said, "all you're trying to do is soak us enough in fines to get back what you spent on these suits."

Instead of exploding at this accusation, Chris thought it was funny. When he finished laughing, he suspended sentence on the three—told them they wouldn't have to pay the fines if they'd promise to behave themselves thereafter.

PRESENT-DAY BALL PARKS all have their "characters" among the fans—individuals, usually, who have developed some peculiar form of rooting. For several seasons, in recent years, Ebbets Field—home grounds for many screwball fans—was graced by the presence of a man who appeared to dislike the Brooklyns. Each time the visiting team scored or executed a double play or got a good hit, this gentleman would cry out, "There goes yer ole baaaall gaaame!" (He seems to have disappeared the last couple of years—probably assassinated.)

Eccentric rooters were not lacking in the earlier days of baseball. In 1900 the New York press took notice of a Polo Grounds rooter who sat in the stands day after day and periodically declaimed in a loud and penetrating voice, "Well! Well!" It is recorded that the management finally barred him from the park on the grounds that his reiteration of "Well! Well!" was making nervous wrecks out of several ballplayers.

During the same period, Brooklyn had to put up with a fan who, day after day, sat in the stands and sang a meaningless song. He sang it steadily, resting only during the minutes in

18

which the teams were changing sides. The lyrics of his song
went:

> *In again and out again;*
> *Out again and in again;*
> *Up again and down again;*
> *Down again and up again.*

During his playing days with Baltimore, John McGraw often
spoke bitterly of a Cleveland fan who pestered him relentlessly
every time the Orioles played at the Ohio city. If McGraw
made an error or struck out or otherwise failed to get a hit, this
individual would leap from his seat, run down to the front walk
of the bleachers, and shout, "Oh, Muggsy! Oh, Muggsy! Look
at your face and see if you ain't a beauty! Oh, Muggsy! Oh,
Muggsy!"

ADRIAN C. ANSON played baseball for twenty-
one years and made the Hall of Fame handily. By
1891, even though he would stay on as an active
player for another five or six years, the sports writers were beginning to hint that Cap was too old for the game. Cap, of
course, thought otherwise, and in September of that year, when
Chicago started a series at Boston, he came onto the field wearing flowing white whiskers and long white hair. He insisted
upon wearing the whiskers throughout the nine-inning contest,
in which he played errorless ball at first base. When he came
to bat for the first time, he turned to Umpire Lynch and announced, "If that ball so much as ruffles these whiskers, I'm
claimin' that I was hit by a pitched ball and takin' my base."
It was a debatable point, and the umpire was just as happy that
Cap's beard was never once disturbed.

IN JUNE of 1911 a man named Patrick Casey sat in a death cell at the Nevada State Penitentiary in Carson City. A couple more days and he would be executed as a murderer.

Casey had been a baseball fan for years and, in fact, had served as an umpire. Now, in the last hours of his life, he could hear the sounds of baseball being played in the prison yard. He listened to these sounds for a while and then asked a guard to call the warden.

"I wonder, Warden," he said, "if you would grant me a last request."

"If it's reasonable—yes," said the warden.

"Before I die," said Patrick, "I'd like to umpire a ball game. Could you have a game tomorrow and let me umpire it?"

The request seemed reasonable to the warden and the ball game was arranged. So, the day before he was to be executed, Casey stood behind the bat. He gave a stirring performance, too, and not once during all the nine innings did any of the convict players dispute his decisions.

THE TWO COMPILERS of this compendium regret that they were unable to attend a series of baseball games at Middletown, New York, during the season of 1889. That was the season in which the team made up of patients from the New York State Homeopathic Hospital for the Insane won eleven games, tied one, and lost only three.

The medical superintendent of the hospital, Dr. Selden H. Talcott, reported at the conclusion of the season that playing baseball was a fine thing for his patients. Said Dr. Talcott:

"The beneficial effects of the national game upon those whose minds have been depressed or disturbed are very marked. The patients in whom it hitherto has been impossible to arouse a healthy interest in anything seem to awaken and become brighter at the sharp crack of the base hit."

IN THE FIRST DECADE of this century the most controversial question in baseball involved the fact that many star pitchers made a practice of spitting on the ball before delivering it. Arguments for and against use of the spitter often grew violent. They sometimes overshadowed discussions of the Boxer Rebellion, the assassination of McKinley, the San Francisco earthquake, and the shooting of Stanford White. Men in high places issued solemn pronunciamentos defending or denouncing the right of a pitcher to spit all over a baseball if he wanted.

Medical men got into the act. For example, Dr. Herman C. H. Herold, president of the Newark Board of Health, announced his opposition to the spitter by saying that a pitcher might have tuberculosis, spit on the ball, and give the disease to the other players.

Others demanded that the spitball be outlawed on aesthetic grounds. President Pulliam of the National League tried to appease these objectors in 1905 by issuing special spitball instructions to his umpires.

The umpires, said President Pulliam, were to watch the pitchers carefully and "see to it that they do not moisten the ball in an ostentatious and objectionable manner, such as holding it a foot or so from the mouth with one hand and licking the fingers of the other hand preparatory to rubbing them on the ball."

If a pitcher prepared his spitter in that vulgar manner, the umpire was to call a balk on him, Mr. Pulliam ordered. If there was such a thing as delicacy in the application of spit to a baseball, the time had come to use it—considering the storm of criticism.

Someone else, discussing the need for a genteel technique, called attention to the methods of Jack Chesbro, known as "king of the spitballers." Chesbro, it was pointed out, "moistens the ball in a way which is entirely free from coarseness, the spectators being unable to see him actually doing it."

During the long controversy which led eventually to the delivery being legislated out of baseball, many pitchers who employed it were interviewed. From those interviews it developed that there were great variations in the technique—details which we will not repeat, since it is our desire to keep vulgarity out of these pages.

One story, however, needs to be mentioned—a widely circulated report that Big Ed Walsh, one of the most famous of the spitball pitchers, chewed "a mysterious substance" while on the mound. When Walsh was finally approached about the matter, he snorted and said there wa'n't nothin' mysterious about it—he simply chewed bark from a slippery ellum.

FORTY AND FIFTY YEARS AGO it was not an uncommon thing for an umpire to carry a loaded revolver on his job—his work was certainly as hazardous as, say, the job of bank guard in the Jesse James country. In 1907, for example, Manager Ducky Holmes of the Lincoln team in the Western League made an official protest against the habits of an umpire named Gifford who always officiated with a pistol in his pocket.

There have been a variety of other cases in which gun-toting umpires figured. Newspapers dated 1896 tell of a ball game in New Jersey between the Clifton and Little Falls teams in which a pitcher named Connelly got angry at the way Umpire Mahoney was calling his serves. Pitcher Connelly got so mad, in fact, that he picked up a bat and started for the umpire. Whereupon Mahoney yanked out his revolver, which he carried in his inside coat pocket. He shoved it into the pitcher's face, telling him at the same time that if he took one more step he'd blow his nose clean through his noggin. Pitcher Connelly, the press reported, returned at once to the mound.

WHEN the hot-stove leaguers get to playing it fast and loose, there's always a good chance that some old-timer will project himself back to 1911 and tell the story which usually begins, "I mind the time when Germany Schaefer stole first base . . ."

Schaefer was playing with Washington against Chicago, and Washington was batting, with the score tied in the ninth. Clyde Milan, a speedster on the base paths, had reached third, and Schaefer was on first. Two men were out, the man at bat was a weak hitter, and there was a desperate need to get Milan across the plate.

On the first pitch Schaefer stole second without an attempt being made to get him. On the next pitch he astounded everybody in the park by dashing back to first and sliding into the bag. His idea had been to draw a throw from the catcher, thereby permitting Milan to score from third. It didn't work, and there was much argument and confusion for a while. Washington finally pulled the game out in the twelfth.

For days, weeks, months—even for years—people talked about that play—always praising Germany Schaefer for inventing a new gimmick in the science of base running. Now the Vice-President in Charge of Research for this book comes along with the information that Schaefer didn't invent the play, that Harry Davis of the Philadelphia Athletics executed the same maneuver nine years earlier and did a better job of it, for Davis succeeded. Whether Germany Schaefer remembered the Davis play or not is a consideration that you may speculate about, if you feel like it.

At any rate, with the situation almost exactly the same, Davis stole second. On the next pitch he went back and stole first. This maneuver confused the Detroit catcher, and the confusion became greater when Davis lit out for second again. This time a throw was made to the shortstop, but Davis arrived safely, and the Philadelphia runner on third crossed the plate.

 "RUBBER STAMP" GRIFFITH was the name they gave the Wichita catcher back in 1915 as a result of a swift play at the plate in a game with Lincoln, Nebraska.

Lincoln players were on second and third when a ball was hit to the outfield. The runner on third stuck to his base, thinking the ball was going to be caught. The man on second saw that the ball would drop in front of the fielder and started running. The two base runners were almost neck and neck as they came down the line. Catcher Griffith squatted in front of the plate, using his shin guards as a sort of barricade. The two runners and the ball all arrived at the same time. As the runners came sliding up against the shin guards, Griffith grabbed the throw and in the manner of a county clerk stamping first the ink pad and then the document tagged out both men.

LITTLE BOYS love baseball. Little boys who love baseball often grow up to continue loving it, thus becoming paying customers. Hence little boys are always given solicitous treatment at the ball parks.

This is a tale of a little boy, identity unknown, who attended a game one day in 1910 at Washington Park, where the Giants were playing Brooklyn.

During the third inning the little boy, seated back of third base, aimed his face in the direction of Arthur Devlin, the big third baseman for the Giants, and cried out in the joyous accents of youth:

"Devlin! Yer a yella dog!"

Mr. Devlin heard it, realized that the voice was that of a child, and playfully stuck his tongue out in the direction of the little boy.

This action offended a gentleman named Philip Schmitt who was occupying a box back of third. Mr. Schmitt and several of his friends now began ascribing the traits of a yella dog to Mr. Devlin. Mr. Devlin replied that he would be over to attend to matters as soon as the inning was finished. Mr. Schmitt and his friends shook their fists at him and cried out, among other things, "You and who else?"

At the end of the inning Mr. Devlin marched to the box, entered it, and began swatting customers as if they were flies. Umpire Bill Klem finally dragged Mr. Devlin away, for now the fans were beginning to converge on the Giants' third base-

25

man. Mr. Klem, in fact, saw fit to hustle Mr. Devlin into the safety of the clubhouse.

Mr. Schmitt and his bruised friends set up a clamor for Devlin's arrest; meanwhile a mob gathered at the clubhouse entrance, crying for Devlin's blood. And Manager John Mc-Graw began arranging a means for his player to escape. McGraw's horseless carriage was brought around, and on signal Mr. Devlin came cautiously through the clubhouse door. The mob surged forward, but a deputy sheriff, bent upon arresting Mr. Devlin, got to him first and grabbed him by the collar. Whereupon Mr. Devlin broke loose and started running. He ran around the clubhouse and around the diamond and around the park, leaping over benches and clambering across a pile of old lumber. After him went the deputy sheriff, and behind the deputy bayed the mob.

The deputy at last caught up with Mr. Devlin, who was hustled into an automobile and hauled off to court where in due course the entire matter was settled amicably.

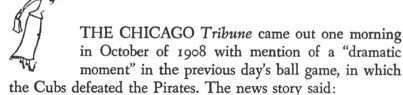

THE CHICAGO *Tribune* came out one morning in October of 1908 with mention of a "dramatic moment" in the previous day's ball game, in which the Cubs defeated the Pirates. The news story said:

"Just as Mordecai Brown swatted the ball bringing in Joe Tinker in the last half of the sixth inning, killing the immediate possibility of a tie game between Chicago and Pittsburgh, and as the crowd in the grandstand rose to cheer, a baby was born far up in the stand in the midst of the dense crowd.

"There is considerable mystery attached to the birth of the 'baseball baby.' The mother fell forward in her seat, and the crowd, thinking she had fainted, moved back to give her air.

"To a woman who raised her head, she told what was happening. Mother and child immediately were carried to the clubhouse, where medical attention was summoned. Then an ambulance was called and both were taken away. The woman refused to give her name."

DURING the first decade of the present century every ballplayer of any consequence had the stage fever. Full-fledged dramatic productions were written as starring vehicles for baseball stars, but most of those who went on the stage chose the medium of vaudeville.

Sports writers complained that many ballplayers had become so preoccupied with their plans for between-season stage appearances that the quality of their play was suffering.

It is recorded, for example, that two Detroit players, Schaefer and O'Leary, spent a good part of their spare moments in the 1907 season rehearsing lines for a vaudeville skit. They had prevailed upon a newspaperman to write a comedy act for them, and they'd sit on the bench practicing dialogue such as this:

> O'LEARY: Have you heard the tale of a baseball?
> SCHAEFER: Don't rib me. A baseball hasn't got a tail.
> O'LEARY: Well, it sure seams sew.
> SCHAEFER: Get to cover.

That is an exact quotation from the script which they were rehearsing.

Of all the great figures in baseball who suffered under theatrical ambition, however, the name of Adrian C. Anson leads the list. As far back as 1887 the stage bug was gnawing at Cap Anson.

That year he brought his Chicago team to New York and one evening Cap went to the theater to see his friends Evans and Hoey perform in a production called *A Parlor Match*.

His actor friends invited him backstage before the start of the performance. They knew of his weakness for the stage and they asked him if he'd like to have a bit part in the show that evening. Of course, said Cap Anson. He was given the role of foreman of a crew of workmen who were digging for some treasure.

When he appeared onstage, one of the workmen was supposed to greet him with the simple salutation, "Good morning." But the workman changed the line to, "Good morning, Captain Anson." The audience whooped, and Cap was so upset that he forgot his line and tried to escape into the wings. The other members of the cast, however, surrounded him and began walloping him with bladders and bouncing sawdust bricks off his head, and the whole thing wound up in an amiable riot.

That experience didn't cure Anson. A few years later, in fact, he was starred in a baseball play called *The Runaway Colt*.

The climax of the play came when the hero (Anson) hit a home run, dashed off into the wings to the right of the stage, on his way to first base, and reappeared soon from the opposite wings to slide for home plate. The actor playing the part of the opposing catcher would receive the ball from somewhere up above and thrust it at the sliding Anson, whereupon the umpire would cry dramatically, "You're safe!" and the final curtain would descend.

One afternoon Anson ran into another of baseball's most colorful characters of the day—Tim Hurst, the fiery umpire.

"Tim," said Cap Anson, "there's nothing on earth like this stage business. You oughta get in it. Why don't you come over tonight and play the umpire part, just for one performance?"

Tim agreed, and that evening's performance of *The Runaway Colt* was remembered and talked about long afterward. For Tim Hurst forgot where he was, or so he said afterward, and as Hero Anson came sliding into the plate on the stage, Umpire Hurst bent forward tensely, saw the ball arrive, saw the actor-catcher slap it on the runner, and just as the curtain started to come down, cried:

"YER OUT!"

OLD-TIME BALLPLAYERS took pride in the extracurricular business of hitting fungos, and many of them developed great skill as sharpshooters. None was better at placing a fungo fly ball than Pat Flaherty of the Chicago White Sox.

Prior to the start of a game one afternoon at the White Sox park, Pat was whacking out fungos to Ducky Holmes in left field. He'd hit the ball to one side and then the other, keeping Holmes galloping, and finally the fielder grew weary and signaled that he'd had enough. Holmes then walked over to the outfield fence, found a shady spot, and sat down to rest.

Flaherty picked up his bat again.

"Look at Ducky out there by the fence," he said to another player. "Watch this one."

He tossed up a ball and gave it a wallop. It rose high in the air, arching its way straight toward Ducky Holmes. Suddenly Flaherty realized that Ducky hadn't been watching and that the ball was probably going to hit him, so he let out a yell of warning. Holmes heard the shout and looked up—just in time to have the ball hit him squarely in the mouth. He was real angry for a while.

ADD TO the hazards of watching a baseball game: eagles.

Eight-year-old Jimmy Pollackson was stretched on the ground watching a game at Port Richmond, Staten Island, one afternoon in 1908.

Suddenly a big American eagle swooped out of the sky and attacked the boy, fastening its claws in his neck. Several men rushed up and pulled the eagle off the boy. Meanwhile Johnny's father ran to his home near by, got a gun, and came back and shot the bird, which had a wingspread of nearly seven feet. The boy was not seriously hurt.

SECOND BASEMAN EGAN of Cincinnati got real furious one afternoon when Joe Tinker of the Cubs executed a vicious slide into second. The two men had words, and Egan challenged Tinker.

"You dirty blank-blank-blank obscenity," said Mr. Egan, "soon as this game's over I'm gonna knock your blank-blank-blank head off!"

Tinker out-blanked him and accepted the challenge. But the Cub shortstop, while being a man of hot temper, usually cooled off rapidly, and by the time the game ended he had forgotten about the dispute. Not so Egan. He waited outside the dressing room and finally invaded the room, only to find that Tinker had just departed.

"He's yella!" cried Egan. "He's run out on me!"

Up spoke Frank Chance, the Cub manager.

"Joe Tinker never ran away from a fight in his life. I'll get him for you."

Chance ran out onto the field and saw Tinker just passing second base, headed for the exit.

"Hey, Joe!" yelled Chance, and Joe turned around just in time to see the bellicose Egan racing toward him, fists clenched. Tinker calmly removed his coat and in a moment the battle was on inside a circle of ballplayers. It lasted perhaps five minutes and witnesses said few men ever took such a beating in that length of time as Egan got from Tinker. And when it was over, Tinker's hair wasn't even ruffled, though unbiased witnesses said he did have to straighten his tie a little.

 ALL OF YOU who have heaped vilification upon the men in blue, called them blind men and thieves and idiots, and urged immediate somatic death upon them—listen to the story of Umpire Day.

The fans in Tacoma, Washington, reached the decision back in 1911 that umpires had been cussed and assaulted enough—it was time that they be given the honor and respect due them; it was time that they be publicly saluted, as a home-run hitter is saluted. So the ninth day of July was designated as Umpire Day. One individual umpire, Jake Baumgarten, was chosen to represent the men of his trade and was assigned to officiate at the day's ball game.

"Today," proudly declared the Tacoma *Ledger*, "is the day when the umpire is received with gladness and joy—even with respect and admiration. It is a day—one in 365—when the indicator-handler at the baseball park will be treated just like we would all want to be treated were we in the same position. It is an exemplification of the Golden Rule—one without a parallel in baseball."

An account in *Sporting Life* of events at the park included the following:

> The spectators, the players, and all spoke kindly to the umpire and even went out of their way to make it plain that they wished to accord him their sincere esteem. The celebration was a complete success. There was no ragging, no display of ill-temper on the part of the players, and the audience showered little courtesies upon the official. The fans entered into the spirit of the thing in a manner which shows that "Umpire Day" can and will be made a great feature in the course of the season's play next year.
>
> Many bouquets were sent out upon the field to the umpire. Most of them were given by stern men who, in the past, had growled their disapproval at decisions which—although fair—had worked against the ultimate success of the home team. At times, when close decisions were made, the usual distasteful disputes were supplemented by such remarks as, "He's out, Mr. Umpire, if you say so," and "Anything you say goes, Mr. Umpire." The afternoon's sport was entirely devoid of any expression of ill-temper.
>
> Prior to the calling of play, the umpire was introduced by State Representative Lorenzo Dow and a fitting little speech followed in which the speaker requested the fans to observe the requirements of the occasion and impressed upon them the fact that they were duty bound to

show their respect and avoid any unpleasant remarks.

At the conclusion of the introductory speech the umpire thanked the audience and shook hands with—and likewise thanked—the players, assuring them of his gratitude toward them. All of this aided in creating a feeling of friendship and kindliness which should at all times exist on the ball field if this great national pastime of ours is to be conducted upon the proper lines to which end will come success and prosperity in a much greater degree than is now the case.

After receiving the flowers, some twenty-odd large floral offerings, the umpire—assisted by the players—carried them to the clubhouse, after which the game proceeded.

As a pretty climax to a most enjoyable afternoon, the umpire stood at the front entrance to the ball park, broke the bouquets and passed out flowers to the ladies as they left the grounds.

A fitting climax to this story would be for us to report that two weeks later Umpire Baumgarten's skull was fractured by a mob of angry fans—but, so far as we know, it didn't happen.

 BIG BILL LANGE, outfielder for Chicago in the 1890s, once won a ball game for his team by lying face downward on the ground.

Chicago had a man on first when Bill came to bat. He hit a single to right field. Rounding first base, he went a bit too far, and the right fielder fired the ball in to the first base-man, making it necessary for Big Bill to dive for the bag. As he came sliding back, the first baseman dropped the ball. Mean-while the other Chicago runner was scampering around the bases. The first baseman couldn't find the ball and Big Bill just lay where he was, half across the bag. The first baseman finally decided that the ball was under Big Bill's immense body and began pulling and tugging, but by the time he did find it the run had scored.

 MALACHI KITTREDGE, catcher for Washing-ton, should have known better. Malachi at least should have known that Willie Keeler was not a ballplayer who spent much time with the etiquette books.

Washington was playing the New York Americans that day in 1903. Willie Keeler, playing then for New York, was on third, and Ganzel was on second. A ground ball was hit to the Washington shortstop, who fired it in to Catcher Kittredge. Keeler had started down for third and now he was trapped as Catcher Kittredge started toward him. Wee Willie surren-dered, gave up. A big smile came on his face and he walked toward Kittredge with his right hand extended.

"Kitt," he said, "I wanna congratulate ya. You're the first catcher ever got me tied up in a mess like this. Nice piece of work, Kitt."

Catcher Kittredge grinned.

"Aw, Willie," he said, relaxing now, "it wasn't really nothin'."

And just then Willie zipped past him. Kittredge whirled and saw that his pitcher was covering the plate. He threw, but the throw hit Wee Willie on the back and bounced to the base of the stands. Gentleman Willie scored, and so did Ganzel.

IN 1912 Germany Schaefer, first-base coach with Washington, devised a little trick through which he could show his contempt for the enemy. Whenever Schaefer was contemptuous of another team's capabilities, he would appear in the coaching box with a bag of popcorn. During the game he would eat the popcorn and gaze at the skies and pretend, generally, that today's contest was a very boresome affair. One day when Schaefer appeared with a huge bag of popcorn during a game against Chicago, Umpire Silk O'Loughlin banished him from the field on the grounds that he was detracting from the dignity of the national pastime. Thus it would appear that Schaefer belongs in the record books —the only big-league player ever expelled from a game for eating popcorn.

MICHAEL (KING) KELLY, for whom the cry of "Slide, Kelly, slide!" was invented, enjoyed nothing so much as rigging a trick play on the diamond. One of his better improvisations came during a game between Chicago and Detroit.

The score was tied as Chicago came to bat in the ninth. Kelly beat out a bunt, and the next man, Ed Williamson, got a base on balls, pushing Kelly down to second.

The two runners now executed a double steal. Kelly made third with a theatrical slide and came off the ground writhing and grimacing with what appeared to be an injured arm. He cried out for the umpire to call time and then, still holding his arm, ran over toward Williamson at second.

"It's thrown out of joint, Ed," he announced loudly. "Take hold of it and pull on it. Easy now."

Then under his breath Kelly spoke quickly to Williamson.

"Keep hold of it, Ed. Nothing wrong with it. Get this, now. On the next pitch I'll start for home. I'll run slow so you can get around third and come in behind me. I want you to be right on my heels as I go in to the plate. Bennett (the Detroit catcher) will try to tag me, and just as he does, I'll spread my legs apart. You dive through my legs for the plate. He can't tag both of us at the same time—one of us is sure to score."

It worked exactly as planned. Bennett tagged Kelly, Kelly spread his legs, Williamson came sliding through, and the run gave Chicago the victory.

BAN JOHNSON, long president of the American League, seemingly had a low opinion of the intelligence of baseball fans. In 1901 he said that the game was getting to be too scientific. "I believe in exciting games," he added, "but the style of play should be limited to the intelligence of the people who pay to see the games."

HAVING achieved fame as a big-league umpire, Silk O'Loughlin decided in 1904 that he'd enter politics.

He ran for the State Assembly on the Democratic ticket that year. On election night a reporter approached him, bringing figures which showed O'Loughlin had been soundly beaten. The reporter asked the noted umpire for a statement.

"I think," said O'Loughlin, grinning, "that the public made a rotten decision."

AN ANGRY MONKEY named Henry disrupted a ball game at Pelican Park in New Orleans one day in 1909. Henry was the mascot of the New Orleans Pelicans and usually was kept tied up near the dugout. Opposing the Pelicans that afternoon was the Mobile team, and the Mobile players began heckling and teasing Henry. The monkey responded, just as a ballplayer would respond, growing angrier and angrier until at last he leaped savagely at a Mobile player and broke the rope which restrained him. Henry went on a rampage through the stands, creating havoc until he was driven away from the field. He perched himself atop the grounds keeper's house and watched the remainder of the game. When it was over he came down and started running around the bases, where he was finally captured.

THE DETROIT management was not happy. At the conclusion of a game, back in 1886, all the Detroit players were called to the box occupied by the club's directors. Three or four of the directors made set speeches. The players would have to put more life into their work, naps on the bench must be discontinued, they were all drawing big salaries for playing ball, and the directors expected each man to do his duty.

At last the players were permitted to leave. Few of them were in a happy mood when they reached their dressing room.

Almost immediately there was a rhubarb. Captain Hanlon instigated it by reprimanding Getzein for his poor performance on the field.

"You go to hell," said Getzein.

"That costs you a twenty-five-dollar fine," said Hanlon.

"You are a son of a bitch," said Getzein.

"Twenty-five dollars more," said Hanlon.

"You are a ————," said Getzein.

"Another twenty-five," said Hanlon.

"You are a ————," said Getzein, getting fancier.

"Twenty-five dollars more."

It kept going like that for a while, until Getzein finally said: "What's it add up to now?"

"Two hundred dollars even," said Hanlon.

"All right," said Getzein. "That's all you are."

 BOSTON was playing at Detroit on the afternoon of May 16, 1909. In the last of the ninth inning Detroit, trailing by one run, worked Moriarty around to third. Two out. Moriarty would have to score to tie it up. He got the signal to steal home and started down the line. The Boston pitcher, however, fired the ball to Catcher Carrigan in perfect position to tag the runner.

Carrigan did tag Moriarty, ending the game. But Carrigan was so contemptuous of Moriarty's foolishness in trying to steal home that, as the runner slid past him, Carrigan casually spat in his face.

Moriarty jumped up and started to swing on the catcher. He saw, in time, that Carrigan had on his mask, so he interrupted the swing, then seized hold of the mask with both hands and jerked it off. Once again he drew back, ready to clout the catcher, but by this time Manager Hughie Jennings arrived on the scene and pulled his man back toward the dugout.

The fans rioted for an hour afterward, surrounding the clubhouse with the intention of waylaying Carrigan. He, however, escaped—disguised in a pair of overalls and a coat belonging to the president of the Detroit club.

THE BEST MANAGERS in baseball are men without sentiment, or, if they have a sentimental side, they have trained themselves to suppress it. In their philosophy the victory's the thing. Yet there have been occasions when even the most case-hardened managers have yielded to the sentimental urge. Even John McGraw.

This story is about James Henry O'Rourke. Forty years ago, if anyone had called him "Mister Baseball," the label would not have been far out of line. He began playing ball at Bridgeport, Connecticut, in 1866. By 1872 he had attracted the attention of Harry Wright, famed manager of the Boston Red Stockings, and Wright signed him on as a first baseman and substitute catcher. In time he became first-string catcher and then, moving over to Providence, was instrumental in that club's winning the National League pennant in 1879.

After playing a few more years at Boston and then at Buffalo, O'Rourke joined the New York Giants. He was playing with Washington when, having reached his late forties, someone decided for him that his big-league career was over.

O'Rourke returned to Bridgeport and in 1896 organized the Connecticut League, serving as secretary-treasurer in the league offices and catching regularly for the Bridgeport club. When he was fifty-four years old he was first-string catcher for Bridgeport as well as the club's owner and secretary of the league. In addition he journeyed out to the ball park each morning and undertook the duties of grounds keeper. He knew the playing field well, for he owned it; the land had been originally a part of his father's farm.

O'Rourke didn't quit regular playing activities until 1909 and he continued for another six years to catch in at least one game each season. Meanwhile he developed his son as a capable player with the Bridgeport club.

One day in September 1904 the New York Giants were to play the Cincinnati Reds, and the game was an extremely important one, for the Giants could clinch the pennant by winning it. Fifteen long years had gone by since the Giants had taken a league championship and O'Rourke had been a member of that old pennant-winning team.

On the day before the game James Henry O'Rourke approached John McGraw and all but begged for the right to get into the Giant line-up, if only for a half inning.

"Jim," said McGraw, "you know you're too old."

"I'm only fifty-two," said O'Rourke.

"It's out of the question," said McGraw. "You ought to know better than to ask."

But O'Rourke didn't give up. He heard that Iron Man McGinnity was to pitch for the Giants the next day and he went to McGinnity and had a talk with him. And McGinnity in turn went to McGraw and talked the manager into letting the fifty-two-year-old veteran enter the game.

Enter it he did, and James Henry O'Rourke didn't play merely half an inning; he played nine full innings in the style of a man half his age and in addition got an important hit for the Giants. McGraw's team won the game—and the pennant—and James Henry O'Rourke went back to Connecticut well satisfied with the flourish he had given his last day as a big-leaguer.

COUNTLESS LEGENDS surround the career of Crazy Schmidt, who was an eccentric's eccentric. Schmidt pitched for many clubs, both in the major and minor leagues, and the early 1890s found him working for the Macon, Georgia, team.

Schmidt got into an altercation with a local fan and wound up in court, charged with throwing a brick at the plaintiff. The judge asked him how he was pleading.

"Not guilty, of course, your honor," said Schmidt. "The fact that the plaintiff is alive today and appears in this court is evidence that I did not throw a brick at him. With the perfect control which I have long demonstrated in throwing baseballs, and which I am sure your honor knows about, if I had thrown a brick at this fellow I would have killed him dead."

Case dismissed.

BASEBALL PLAYERS in time developed their own weapons to use against spitball pitching. The most effective device appears to have had its origin in Pittsburgh in 1912 when the Phillies came in for a series with the Pirates. Pittsburgh had just recently acquired a star spitball pitcher named Marty O'Toole. The Phillies knew that O'Toole would be pitching against them, and it was the Philadelphia first baseman, Fred Luderus, who figured out a way to defeat O'Toole. It was a simple plan, though not quite so simple as feeding crackers to the spitball pitcher just before game time.

The Phillies had seen O'Toole in action and were acquainted

with his technique. He held the ball up to his face, hiding it with his glove, and licked it with his tongue.

So First Baseman Luderus simply equipped himself with a small tube of powerful liniment and whenever he got his hands on the ball he applied some of that liniment to the cover. Before long O'Toole's tongue was on fire, and he was in such pain that he had to withdraw. The trick was quickly discovered, and after the initial shrieking had died away formal statements were issued, including one by Manager Fred Clarke of Pittsburgh, who denounced the Phillies one and all.

"This liniment," he said, "is the most powerful known. Suppose a man should get a little of it on his hand and rub his hand over his eye—he would be rendered blind for hours."

The gold-plated cuspidor, however, was awarded to Manager Red Dooin for his statement in which he accepted responsibility in the matter. The liniment was put on the ball by his order, he said, not for the purpose of making O'Toole's tongue hurt, but to protect the health of his players.

"That ball," he said, "may be carrying the germs of any one of many contagious diseases. So we put disinfectant on it whenever we face a spitball pitcher. I do not deny it, and I'm not afraid to say that we are going to continue to do so. I do not see how we can be refused the privilege of protecting ourselves."

NATIONAL LEAGUE managers in 1881 didn't have much to work with in the way of spare players. The official roster for that year contained eighty-eight names, eleven men being listed for each of the eight clubs. Each team had two pitchers and two catchers and only one man for each of the fielding positions. If a fielder got hurt or put out of the game or turned up drunk, then the spare pitcher went in to take his place. And there were instances where the spare catcher was called upon to pitch.

THERE was never any telling what those Baltimore Orioles would do to win a ball game.

Joe Kelly was playing the outfield for the Orioles one afternoon in the 1890s. A high wind had hit the city on the preceding night, and the fence at Kelly's back had been knocked over. By the time the game started, workmen had succeeded in getting the fence partially back into position. At one point, however, it was still sloping outward at a forty-five-degree angle.

Early in the game a hard-hit ball soared over Kelly's head. He turned and raced after it. Reaching the base of the sloping fence, Kelly twisted his head and saw that the ball would still be out of his reach. He didn't even slow down, but ran right up the slope. Just as he reached the top the ball slapped into his glove, and the momentum of his rush carried him clear out of the park.

It was, possibly, the only time a fair ball was hit over the fence for an out instead of a home run.

AMONG the freak home runs of baseball history none has ever evoked more scientific discussion than "the grounder that clumb over the wall" at the Brooklyn ball park in 1916.

The Dodgers were playing Philadelphia, and the score was tied as Brooklyn came to bat in the last of the eleventh.

George Cutshaw, the Dodger second baseman, hit a sizzling line drive just inside the right-field foul line. Let us now turn the story over to a sports writer on the Brooklyn *Eagle* who was present.

"Cutshaw's whack should have gone to the concrete wall and it should have been good for anywhere from one to three bases, according to the carom. It landed on a hard spot near the foul line and a foot or two from the concrete. It bounded up, and up, following the wall, which had a slight incline away from the field. It literally climbed over, pausing a moment on the top to give the laugh to Right-fielder Cravath.

"How the climb was made, and what peculiarity of 'English' was imparted to the ball when it first landed on the ground, will never be explained by a finite mind."

 CHARLIE O'LEARY, who played with Detroit for many years, once was reminiscing about the joy that comes to a busher when he finally achieves that great ambition to become a major leaguer.

After proving himself in the minors, success finally came for Charlie when he was signed on by the Chicago White Sox. His heart was pounding and his happiness was without bounds on that great day when he joined the club in Detroit.

Charlie got to play briefly that first day, and the White Sox, after a bitter contest, won from Detroit by a single run. The Detroit fans were unhappy about the outcome of the game.

When the Chicago players left the park they were greeted with a hail of beer bottles. They scrambled for a bus, got inside it, and all stretched out on the floor of the vehicle as it moved off through a bombardment of rocks and bottles.

Charlie admitted later that he was a scared rookie and that he stayed on the floor of the bus all the way to the hotel. He told an older player that he didn't like the experience one bit.

"Hell, son," said the veteran, "don't let this worry you. It happens to us nearly every day. You'll get used to it in a week or two."

THE SCORE on umpires for one week of the season of 1901:

The Giants refused to play in any game to which Umpire Nash was assigned, so Nash was dismissed by the National League.

Umpire Cunningham was mobbed by fans at Pittsburgh after a player protested one of his decisions by throwing the ball over the grandstand.

Several Baltimore players assaulted Umpire Sheridan at Detroit.

Catcher Wilson of Montreal flattened Umpire Hunt.

Umpire Cunningham was knocked down by a player at Cincinnati.

THE ANTICS of Hughie Jennings on the coaching lines during his years as Detroit manager brought vast amusement to the Detroit fans and sometimes got Jennings into trouble with the umpires.

It's a dubious distinction, but Hughie is said to have introduced the fingers-in-the-mouth whistle into the repertoire of the nation's baseball coaches. Previously he had employed a gymnastic exercise in which he stood on one leg, lifted his arms above his head, and screeched something which sounded like "Eeeeee-yah!" He delivered this cry with such shrill vigor that one day in 1907 he warped his vocal apparatus. Finding himself temporarily unable to "Eeeeee-yah!" effectively, Hughie turned up on the coaching lines with a postman's whistle.

The whistle soon had the nerves of Umpire Silk O'Loughlin on edge, and the umpire ordered that Jennings desist.

"Kindly show me," roared Hughie, "anything in the rule book that says it's illegal to toot on a policeman's whistle!"

Hughie persisted in blowing the whistle whenever a Detroit man got on base, whereupon O'Loughlin bounced him out of the game and suspended him for ten days. Jennings took his case to President Ban Johnson, but the league president ruled against him. It was then that Hughie began using his two middle fingers to produce sounds that were, if anything, more ear-piercing than any postman's whistle.

The finger whistle, then, became one of Hughie's trademarks, but he had others. He resumed his one-leg stand and "Eeeeee-yah!" cry, and he developed a habit of bending down and plucking grass, possibly as a signal.

In 1912, between playing seasons, Hughie got involved in an automobile accident. His back, left leg, and right hand were injured, and it looked as though he would have to abandon his grass-plucking, one-leg stands and tricky finger whistle.

Some of the umpires, figuring the crash might turn Jennings into a sedate and comparatively silent coach, openly referred to it as an Act of God. But they did not reckon with the comeback ability of the Tiger manager who, years earlier, had survived a running dive into a concrete swimming pool from which the water unexpectedly had been drained. When the next season rolled around, Jennings again was giving with noise and acrobatics on the coaching lines.

AMONG the many remarkable eccentrics who have decorated the diamond at one time or another, Pete Browning, who was a star batsman for Louisville in the old American Association, certainly ranks high.

Browning, for example, apparently was the father of one of the oldest and corniest gag devices known to man. He and a teammate were sitting in a hotel lobby when the news came that President Garfield had been shot.

"That's awful!" said Pete's teammate.

"What's awful?" Pete wanted to know.

"Garfield has been shot."

"Gee," said Pete, "that's too bad. I didn't know him, I guess. What league was he in?"

Browning was a nut about the bats he used. At the end of each season he took them to his home and submitted them to a complicated routine, soaking them in a water trough. Each bat, he said, required a definite period of soaking, some staying in the water a month, some half that long, some only a few days.

BALTIMORE fans took their baseball seriously sixty years ago. Quite often when they were dissatisfied with the way things were going they swarmed onto the field swinging fists, bottles, and clubs. A sort of climax was achieved one afternoon in 1884 when Louisville was playing Baltimore. The umpire was assaulted, and after that the Baltimore club's secretary was knocked down. On the following day a stout barbed-wire fence was erected around the diamond, separating the fans from the playing field.

 TWO SEMI-PRO TEAMS were playing at Monroe Center, Illinois, on a June day in 1901. During the early innings the sky grew dark with clouds and lightning began flashing, but no rain was falling, so the contest continued. In the last half of the seventh Morris Carlson was crouched at his position on first base, awaiting the next pitched ball. Suddenly there was a blinding flash of lightning. Carlson raised his hands to his chest, spun around, and fell to the ground. He was dead when his teammates reached his side.

 BASEBALL is a democratic institution. One of the authors of this book once sat in a baseball park and saw a foul ball go into the field boxes and hit James A. Farley smack on his bald spot. This, mind you, when Mr. Farley was chairman of the Democratic National Committee—not just a soft-drink salesman. No matter how important a man may be to his valet, he has to duck with the rest of them when he gets into a ball park.

The point is nicely illustrated in the report of a game in which Minneapolis played Kansas City at Kansas City on September 10, 1909.

The umpire that day was Clarence Owens, a conscientious official, and there came a point in the contest when the home team was about to get a big batting rally going. Umpire Owens called a Kansas City player out at first on a close play. Immediately a messenger came onto the field and informed Mr. Owens that "Mr. Sherman would like to speak to you in his box."

Umpire Owens walked over to the box where James S. Sherman, Vice-President of the United States, was seated.

"Mr. Owens," said Mr. Sherman, "I believe your decision on that play was incorrect. The man was safe. Your umpiring has been good up to this point, but I am convinced that you made a mistake in this particular instance."

Umpire Owens reflected a moment.

"Well, Mr. Sherman," he said, "it's quite possible that I did make a mistake. You know, baseball is a good deal different kind of business than running the government. Folks in the baseball business do sometimes make errors. But back there in Washington, where they make the laws and run the government, they never make any mistakes."

Vice-President Sherman seemed perplexed at first over this unexpected response. Then he broke into laughter and shook hands with Umpire Owens and told him to go on back to his job and forget about what any spectator might have to say to him.

ONE AFTERNOON in 1893 a young man named Thomas Maddigan was playing in the field for a Pittsburgh team. Suddenly he quit his post and came limping in to the bench. He said that he had just been hit by a batted ball and was hurt. He looked sick, yet his teammates knew that he had not been hit by anything—no ball had gone anywhere near him.

Young Maddigan went home and got into bed. Doctors could find nothing wrong with him, yet he insisted that he was badly hurt. He refused to get out of bed, and he stayed there six long years. At the end of that time he was twenty-eight years old, and the hallucination had become more pronounced, if anything. In 1899 he was adjudged to be hopelessly insane and was removed to a hospital for the mentally deranged.

 ONE SATURDAY AFTERNOON back in 1905 the New York Giants were playing in the City of Brotherly Love.

In the eighth inning a Giant player named McGann came tearing toward the plate, trying to score. Abbott, the Philadelphia catcher, tagged the runner out by ramming the ball into his ribs. McGann promptly swung a roundhouse right to the pit of Abbott's stomach. Abbott retaliated by throwing the ball as hard as he could, hitting McGann in the back. They were clawing at each other when the umpire intervened and banished them from the field.

That wasn't so much. There was more to come. In the ninth a lemonade peddler, forgetting his business affairs for the moment, began screeching dirty names at a Giant pitcher. The Giant responded by walloping the peddler in the mouth, whereupon the huckster began beating the ballplayer on the head with his lemonade tray. The Giant, drenched with lemonade and wearing knots on his head, resumed play after the peddler had been expelled from the park.

There was more to come. As the last out was made, the Philadelphia fans came roaring out of the stands, bent upon bloodletting. The Giant players barely reached their carriages ahead of the mob. All along Huntington Street and later on

Broad the fans pursued the carriages, showering bottles, bricks, and rocks onto the heads of the New Yorkers, while the drivers lashed their horses furiously.

No one was seriously hurt—seriously, by the standards of the times.

 DURING a game Baltimore was playing at Chicago many years ago Umpire Joe Cantillon called several plays which gave the contest to the visitors. Consequently, Mr. Cantillon became extremely unpopular with the Chicago players as well as the fans.

The following day the umpire arrived at the entrance gate to the park, accompanied by two friends. He wanted to have his friends passed in free, but the gateman insisted they would have to pay.

"Go ask Comiskey about it," said Umpire Cantillon, and the gateman obeyed. He located Charles Comiskey, boss of the Chicago team, and laid the matter before him.

"Well, well, well," said Comiskey. "So an umpire claims he has two friends! Let him bring them into the park by all means. If he has any friends at all, he ought to be permitted to keep them with him at all times. He might need them."

THERE ARE many individuals in this country who look upon baseball as a boresome game, altogether lacking in exciting incident. It is all but impossible to explain to these people such a scene as met the eye when the American League season opened in Chicago back in 1900. A contemporary account relates:

"The grounds are still in a state of roughness, with lakes in the outfield. On the fence at the rear sat several painters, busy daubing white paint upon the boards. These honest men had hard work to watch the game and paint at the same time. They grew wildly enthusiastic, and when the hits came thick they flopped their paint cans against the wall and dropped their brushes. Later, when it looked as though Chicago would win, they grabbed their brushes and began painting each other in wild delight."

RAYVILLE was playing Vidalia down in Louisiana one afternoon in 1907. The two teams appeared to be pretty evenly matched in the early innings, and then Rayville sent its new pitcher into the game—man by the name of Lee.

He struck out the first batter to face him. Then he struck out the second batter. He had fanned his seventh consecutive man and was about to go to work on number eight. The Vidalia men on the bench were understandably chagrined. By this time, in fact, they were behaving in a manner quite strange to the locale—cursing a man named Lee. Suddenly one of the Vidalia players leaned forward, took a long look at the enemy, and let out a roar.

"Hell's farr!" he yelled. "That's the perfesser."

And so it was. The man on the mound was Professor Leo Lee, an itinerant hypnotist.

"He's bin a hip-muhtizin' us!" screamed the men of Vidali, carrying their case straight to the umpire. The "perfesser" tried to protest that he had not been employing his hypnotic powers on the batters—that he was unable to hypnotize a person except when he was in a tent. Somebody popped somebody else on the

54

nose. In a moment fists were flying, and in another moment men were whopping each other with bats. When the fighting was over, the game was called "no contest" and the Rayville manager was notified that in the interests of his personal health it would not be advisable for him to ever use "Perfesser" Lee again in those parts.

JOHN KILLACKEY played his regular position at second base for the Paterson club in a game with Newark on May 29, 1896. John was afield, that is, during the first inning.

At the end of that inning someone came to John on the bench and told him he was wanted around at the side of the grandstand. The Paterson infielder walked around the structure and suddenly was confronted by his sins.

A constable was there, bearing a warrant for the arrest of John Killackey. And the complaining party, Miss Kate Cameron, stood beside the constable. It appears that Miss Cameron had traveled all the way to Newark from Cleveland to make Killackey marry her—or else.

Hot words were passed, and finally Killackey announced that he would rot in jail before he married the girl. The constable promptly informed him that jail was where he would rot if he didn't marry her. The conference continued for a while, and Killackey cooled somewhat. Before long he and Miss Cameron were on better terms, and then he agreed to marry her.

Someone went into the stands and found a justice of the peace named Sturtevant and brought him around. The happy couple was escorted to a secluded corner, and in a few moments the ceremony was over. The newspaper reports of the wedding make no mention of firearms, though it is likely that the constable was packing a gun.

PRESIDENT CHARLES W. ELIOT of Harvard had a low opinion of baseball. In the 1880s Dr. Eliot sputtered:

"I think baseball is a wretched game; but as an object of ambition for youth to go to college for, really it is a little weak. There are only nine men who can play the game, and there are nine hundred and fifty men in college; and out of those nine there are only two desirable positions, I understand—pitcher and catcher—so there is but little chance for the youth to gratify his ambition. I call it one of the worst games, although I know it is called the American national game."

(If the above quotation seems to read wretchedly, try it with a Harvard accent.)

THERE WERE OCCASIONS in the rugged days of baseball when umpires sometimes chose *not* to see certain happenings on the diamond.

Philadelphia was playing the Baltimore Orioles at Baltimore one April day in 1895. Two umpires, Murray and Campbell, were officiating.

At one point in the game the Philadelphia pitcher, Taylor, somehow got back to cover second base just as Hughie Jennings, the Baltimore shortstop, came charging down from second. Jennings appeared to do a deliberate job of ramming into Pitcher Taylor with his shoulder, knocking Taylor to the ground. Taylor promptly got up and clouted Jennings on the jaw, knocking *him* down.

"Did you see anything?" Umpire Murray asked of Umpire Campbell.

"Nope. Did you?"

"Nope."

"Well, then, let's get on with the ball game."

A GAME of baseball was in progress near a railroad roundhouse at Pitcairn, Pennsylvania, back in 1906. One of the batters hit a long foul fly down the left-field line and B. F. Hicks, the left fielder, raced after it. In order to get to the ball, Hicks had to run up an embankment and onto a railroad spur. The instant he caught the ball a locomotive struck him and killed him. When his companions reached his side they found the ball still clutched in his hand.

THE CRY of "You robber!" has always been one of the most common taunts directed against umpires, though it rarely has signified the belief that an umpire has been guilty of actual stealing.

Bill Klem, one of the great personalities of big-league umpiring, was once accused of petty larceny on the baseball diamond. It happened after a game in Boston, and the accuser was Fred Tenney, manager of the Boston Nationals.

Tenney came up to Klem after the game and demanded the right to search the umpire.

"What for?" asked Klem.

"Baseballs," said Tenney. He then accused Klem of stealing baseballs by simply not turning them in after each game.

Umpire Klem promptly belted Mr. Tenney in the jaw. Mr. Tenney struck Umpire Klem in the jaw, and Umpire Klem then struck Mr. Tenney somewhat harder in the jaw. There the matter ended.

BACK IN THE 1880s, when the rules of baseball were not too stringent, an outfielder didn't necessarily have to trudge all the way in to the bench each inning. If he felt that he would not be needed as a batter, he could go back to the fence and sit down and wait until it was time for him to take the field again. Moreover, he was allowed to entertain visitors during those inactive moments.

All of which is preliminary to the story of Abner Dalrymple's catch. Yes, Abner Dalrymple. Abner was an outfielder for Chicago, and late in the season of 1885 his team was in a close race with Philadelphia for the pennant.

Philadelphia met Chicago in an important series, and the first game of the series went into extra innings. After a time it began to get dark, but the struggle continued with the score tied. In the top half of the fourteenth Chicago scored a run and broke the tie. In its half Philadelphia got men on second and third, with two out and a good hitter at the plate. Abner Dalrymple was at his post in left field. Suddenly the man at the plate, who seemingly had the eyes of an owl, swung hard in the twilight, and the ball took off. By this time it had grown so dark that everyone in the park lost sight of the ball

—everyone except Abner Dalrymple. Abner raced toward the left-field fence, turned finally, leaped high in the air, and made what appeared to be a beautiful catch for the game-ending third out. Through the murk the spectators saw him stuff the ball into his hip pocket and run off the field.

There were some who suspected Abner Dalrymple of funny business—some who believed he didn't see that ball at all, but merely pretended that he saw it and caught it and shoved it in his hip pocket. Yet nobody could prove a thing. It was argued down through the years.

Then, some fifteen years later, a Salt Lake City man named Hopkins told his story. He had been "visiting" with Abner in the outfield that day. He had been sitting out there against the fence in left field all afternoon.

"I can tell you," said Hopkins, "that Abner Dalrymple *did* see that ball, because I saw it. It went at least ten feet over the fence."

LITTLE JOHN McGRAW was described many times as fearing no man. One day he announced that he was growing tired of these tributes to his courage. During a bull session he confessed that on one occasion, at least, he got so scared that he felt his backbone begin to curl.

Back in the 1890s McGraw had a side job of coaching a college team in Maryland, and one afternoon his boys played a team from the Spring Grove Asylum—a team composed entirely of mental patients.

It was an exciting game, McGraw recalled, and was tied up in the ninth inning.

"A lunatic was on second base," McGraw said, "and another one, a big strong fellow named Berg, was at bat. I was standing near our bench."

Suddenly Berg dropped his bat and started running in McGraw's direction. It was then that the Little Napoleon's knees began to clatter. He just stood there, waiting for the assault, but Berg ran right past him, heading for the left-field fence, with a number of asylum attendants in close pursuit.

Later on McGraw asked one of the attendants what had caused the man to act as he did.

"That poor fellow," said the attendant, "is sane in every way until he sees a chicken. He is afraid of chickens, and when he was standing at the plate he happened to look up and see a chicken out beyond right field. So he simply went to pieces and took off in the opposite direction."

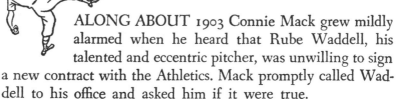

ALONG ABOUT 1903 Connie Mack grew mildly alarmed when he heard that Rube Waddell, his talented and eccentric pitcher, was unwilling to sign a new contract with the Athletics. Mack promptly called Waddell to his office and asked him if it were true.

"Yeh," said Rube. "I don't wanna sign the contract."

"You mean you don't think I'm paying you enough?" asked Mack.

"No," said Rube. "It ain't the salary that's botherin' me. I won't sign no contract 'less it says that damn Schreckengost quits eatin' them damn crackers in bed."

Mack then got the story out of Waddell. The Rube and Schreckengost were roommates. They got along well except for Schreckengost's habit of taking a box of crackers to bed with him and eating them before he went to sleep. Since Rube usually had to sleep in the same bed, he complained that the crumbs drove him crazy, and he wasn't going to put up with it any more. He wanted it in the contract.

So Connie Mack inserted a clause which said that if Waddell's roommate ever ate crackers in bed the Rube would be given a change of quarters.

THERE'S an economic factor in the tendency of certain fans to throw pop bottles at umpires. This was proven back in 1906 by Charles Comiskey, owner of the Chicago White Sox. Comiskey put his mind to work on the problem after Umpire Billy Evans had been the target for a shower of bottles from the bleachers near first base. Comiskey decided that a fan who paid only twenty-five cents for his seat was a potential bottle-thrower, while a fan who paid fifty cents had greater dignity and would rarely, if ever, let go with a bottle. Accordingly Comiskey upped the price of seats opposite the base lines to fifty cents. That left only the bleachers in deep center field in the cheaper class. "Out there," said Comiskey, "they can throw their arms off and bother no one."

PONDEROUS FILES in the United States Patent Office show clearly that the inventors of our nation have not completely ignored baseball.

One of the more outlandish contrivances is described as a "baseball catcher" under Patent Number 755,209. "My invention," says the patenting genius, "relates to certain new and useful improvements in devices to be used by catchers and other players to protect their hands, the same being so constructed as to receive and retain the ball without the players' hands coming in contact therewith."

The device is pictured as a box made of wood and heavy wire and built to reach from the player's chin to his waist. Two wire doors, hinged to the side of the box and swinging inward, form the front of the contraption. At the top is a wire screen to protect the player's face.

To catch the ball the player would have to do nothing more than get the box in front of the oncoming sphere. The ball, striking the swinging doors, would enter the box and thud against a pad backed up by springs. Then it would drop through a pipe attached to the bottom of the box. The bottom of this pipe would be closed, but there would be a side hole through which the player could slip his hand and grab the ball.

This contrivance was patented chiefly for the use of catchers, but the inventor neglected to consider how it might be used in handling high fouls. Obviously, the catcher would first have to get under the descending ball, then flop himself flat on his back in order to present his swinging doors to the sky.

Fielders who might object to galloping around with big boxes strapped to their bodies could turn to the product of another inventive genius's mind. This man devised and patented a large funnel-shaped dingbat which would be strapped to the player's forearm. The ball would enter the funnel, where a mechanical ejector would swiftly flip it back into the air, so the player could get his hands on it.

Thirty-odd varieties of mechanical pitchers have been patented, employing centrifugal force, springs, catapults, compressed air, and mastodonic rubber bands—everything, in fact, but gunpowder.

Patent Number 1,083,338, issued in 1914, is a device for the use of human pitchers. It calls for a leather gear resembling a football player's shoulder rig. Leading over the shoulder and down the pitching arm is an elastic band anchored to a strap at the wrist—the entire affair looking like a piece of hospital equipment for a patient with a badly broken arm. The purpose behind this gadget: "to relieve the arm from the shock incurred when a ball is suddenly released in the act of throwing."

Patent Number 1,868,088 was granted to a man interested in reducing the margin of error for umpires. The patent calls for a motor, an elongated light bulb, and an electric fan to be buried beneath home plate. Two slots, one on each side, would be cut in the plate itself. Beneath these slots would be lenses through which light from the buried lamp would be projected. During a ball game the umpire would go into a low squat back of the plate. If, as the ball arrived, he saw light reflected on its lower surface, then he would know for certain that it had passed directly over the plate. And why the electric motor and fan? To keep a stream of air moving across the lenses so no dust would get on them.

Yet another boon to the business of umpiring is found in an invention which employs the principle of the roller towel. A clean white sheet of paper would cover home plate, and the moment it got soiled the umpire would step up, pull a clean sheet across the plate, and rip off the old. Do away with whisk brooms.

The use of bases that whistle piercingly when touched by a player's foot is mentioned elsewhere in this book. There also have been inventions patented in which an underground bell would clang when the base is nudged. The inventor who was granted Patent Number 172,315, however, came up with a bell inside the ball itself—the exact purpose being unclear to the non-technical minds of your correspondents.

Among other noteworthy inventions is a bat shaped like a question mark which, the inventor asserted, would do away with foul balls; and a rubber contrivance worn on the hand which would simplify the business of pitching "incurves, outcurves, upshoots, or downshoots."

ONE DAY in July of 1909 James Phelps was playing in the outfield for Rayville in a game at Monroe, Louisiana.

In the eighth inning a Monroe batter drove a long fly over Phelps's head. He turned with the crack of the bat and raced into a bog on the outer edge of the playing field, and the spectators roared approval when he made a spectacular one-handed catch of the ball.

At the moment the ball hit his glove Phelps felt a stinging sensation on his leg. Glancing down, he saw a large snake. He was one of the team's star players, and he felt that he should stay in the game, so he said nothing about the snake and played out the ninth inning. Only then did he mention the snake to his teammates. Two hours later he was dead.

THE FACT that actors are sometimes accorded special privileges around baseball parks has evoked bitter feeling even in our own time. Back in the 1890s an actor's presence at a Boston game brought on a lot of confusion and affected the outcome of the contest.

The actor was Harry Dixey, an avid baseball fan. Dixey didn't sit in the stands with the common herd, but arrived

each day in a fancy buckboard which he would drive to a spot in deep left field.

He was sitting in his rig out there one afternoon when Chicago was playing Boston. Beside the actor was his pet bull terrier.

In the third inning a slugger named Dahlen belted a long drive to left, far over the fielder's head. The ball struck Dixey's bull terrier in the head, killing him, and then bounced out of the buckboard and fell beneath the feet of the horses. Up came the left fielder, but when he made an effort to retrieve the ball the horses got excited and started rearing and kicking. The actor, already sort of bereaved, was thrown from his rig, and the rig itself was wrecked by the flying hoofs.

Other over-all consequences: Slugger Dahlen got a home run; Actor Dixey thereafter sat in the stands.

GERMANY SCHAEFER, second baseman for Detroit, had a great reputation for daffiness. One day he got into an argument with his Tiger team-mate, Davey Jones, who also was his roommate. Schaefer was insisting that the earth does not revolve and said he could prove it.

"I knowed you was crazy," said Davey, "but not that crazy."

"I said I can prove it and I can," argued Schaefer, and they made a bet. That night in their hotel room Schaefer filled a bathtub with water and called Davey in and told him to look at it. When they got up the next morning Schaefer took his roommate by the arm, led him again to the bathroom, and showed him the tub, still filled with water.

"Now," said Schaefer, "it stands to reason that if the earth revolved during the night, as they say, then that water would have spilled outa the tub."

"By God, Germany," said Davey Jones, "I never thought of it that way. You win."

OCCUPYING a prominent shelf position in the private library of Mr. Fred Allen is an ancient book which Mr. Allen picked up one day for thirty-five cents. The title of the book is *Never Hit a Man Named Sullivan*, and it attracted Mr. Allen's eye for the reason that his true name is John F. Sullivan. He has never read the inside part of it—he's satisfied with the title.

There is a baseball story about a man named Sullivan, an umpire who served in the Eastern League back in 1907. During a game between Rochester and Jersey City, Umpire Sullivan found himself embroiled with a hotheaded pitcher named Foxen. Mr. Foxen called Mr. Sullivan a vast variety of badword names, and in the end the umpire ordered the pitcher out of the game, off the field, and off the earth.

Mr. Foxen, however, wasn't finished. Instead of leaving the park, he quietly procured a baseball bat. Then he went to the dressing room assigned to the umpire and waited for the game to end.

When the unsuspecting umpire stepped into his dressing room, Foxen quickly followed him, closed the door and locked it. Then, with the bat in his hands, he announced that he was going to beat Mr. Sullivan to a pulp.

Horrible noises were soon heard coming from the room, and someone called the police. They broke into the dressing room, fearing they would find Umpire Sullivan dead or dying. Instead they found that Mr. Sullivan had taken the bat away from Mr. Foxen and then, using only his fists, was beating Mr. Foxen to a pulp. Mr. Foxen was hauled off to jail but Umpire Sullivan decided against pressing charges, and that was the end of it—save that Mr. Foxen never again hit a man named Sullivan.

EDWARD HEIM, who had been a star pitcher for Princeton in 1905, lost his life by drowning at Coney Island. When he was "laid out" for burial, a baseball was placed in his right hand and went with him to the grave.

BACK IN 1895, when Charles Comiskey was running the ball club in St. Paul, he was sitting in the stands watching a game when a big thought came into his head.

"My goodness!" he said to himself, "just look at all the left-handed batters we got!" He counted them to make sure and found that seven of the St. Paul regulars batted left-handed. "Well, bless my soul!" said Mr. Comiskey.

So it was that when the team went on the road a few days later Mr. Comiskey led a gang of workmen into his park and proceeded to reconstruct it so that it would better suit the talents of a team composed largely of lefties. The diamond was shifted so that the right-field foul line crossed the fence just a few yards beyond first base. In order to achieve this, third base had to be moved a long way from its old location and ended up at a stop where a man standing on the base could almost reach out and touch the front of the left-field bleachers.

And what does a man get for being clever? Nasty criticism—that's what—and Mr. Comiskey got so much of it that he had to change everything back to the way it had been.

 AMERICAN LEAGUERS of 1904 often complained that whenever they met the Chicago White Sox on their home grounds, they usually had to play against not only the ball team but the entire city. The fervor of the Chicago fans is illustrated by the following newspaper account of a contest between the White Sox and the Philadelphia Athletics:

> Rube Waddell was pitching for the Athletics and was making monkeys out of the White Sox batters, with his team well ahead in the scoring as the game went into the closing innings.
>
> The contest had drawn a large crowd, spectators standing around the playing field. In the ninth inning the White Sox staged a great rally. It looked as though one more White Sox hit would send Rube out of the game. With affairs in that state, Callahan lifted a high foul fly a few feet back of the plate. The Philadelphia catcher started back for it but he was due to have a lot of trouble in making the catch. Small boys rushed into his path, some of them literally throwing themselves against his legs. To top it all, a

grandstand patron threw a cushion which hit the struggling catcher. Despite all that, he managed to get to the ball and made the catch.

The next batter hit a long foul down the left-field line where the crowd was massed. Earlier in the game, whenever the Philadelphia batters hit long fouls like that, the crowd had opened up to let the Chicago outfielders make the catch. On this foul fly, however, the spectators held a solid front against the efforts of Topsy Hartsel, the Philadelphia left fielder, to reach the ball.

Rube Waddell managed to strike out the batter with the next pitch, however, and the game was over with the Athletics chalking up a victory which certainly was hard earned.

 A COURT CASE which should be of interest to all baseball fans, not to mention spectators at other events, appeared on the docket in Atlanta back in 1909.

R. C. Buie, a spectator at a ball game in Atlanta, placed his feet on the back of the seat in front of him. The occupant of that seat, Edward Maddox, turned around and suggested that the Buie feet be placed somewhere else. Buie told Maddox to go take a flying jump at a galloping goose. Maddox then hauled off and belted Buie in the nose.

Maddox was taken into court charged with assault and battery. The judge listened to the evidence. Then he ruled: defendant was justified in striking plaintiff. Case dismissed.

AT THE POLO GROUNDS one afternoon in 1898, when the Giants were engaged against Baltimore, a Baltimore batter named Ducky Holmes was fanned. From the stands came a taunting cry:

"Ducky, you are a lobster!"

Ducky disliked being called a lobster, whirled around, and uttered a few choice obscenities in response. These were overheard by President Freedman of the New York club. Mr. Freedman tried to get the Baltimore manager to yank Holmes out of the game. Request refused. Mr. Freedman next asked the umpire to remove Holmes. Request refused. Mr. Freedman then called on the police to seize Holmes and throw him out of the park. Request refused. Mr. Freedman then said, dagnabbit, his team wouldn't play another lick if that foul-mouthed Holmes weren't taken out.

With the Giants under orders not to play, the game was forfeited to Baltimore as of the fourth inning. The Baltimore manager insisted that his club be given its share of the gate receipts. The money was handed over. Then the fans started howling— and President Freedman could do nothing but refund their money. He not only lost heavily on the deal, but as he was leaving the park someone yelled at him:

"Freedman, you are a lobster!"

EDUCATED PEOPLE know that when a ball lands in fair territory, between home plate and first base or between home plate and third base, and then rolls outside the foul line, that ball is a foul.

In one celebrated instance, however, the rule did not hold—not in the opinion of Tim Hurst, whose umpiring contributed greatly to the color of the American League contests in the early days. Umpire Hurst, in fact, ruled on such a play with one of the most remarkable judicial utterances ever heard on a baseball field.

Sam Crawford, the Detroit star, was at bat against Washington one July afternoon in 1906. The score was tied 3 to 3, and the game had reached the seventh inning. Crawford swung hard at a pitch that was shoulder high. The ball went almost straight up a tremendous distance, and Wakefield, the Washington catcher, couldn't seem to locate it. At last it came down and hit the ground about a foot in front of home plate. It was spinning as it hit and bounced back over the plate and rolled to the stands. Crawford ran down to first, and meantime two other Detroit runners crossed the plate.

The Washington players swarmed around Tim Hurst after he had called it a fair ball. They screamed and cursed and poked index fingers violently against his chest, but he folded his arms and stood by his guns. They shouted the text of the official rule at him, and he said yes, he knew that rule, and then he delivered his historic explanation:

"It went too high in the air. It couldn't be a foul."

 LARRY McLEAN, a capable catcher, was a ball-player who had whisky trouble. In 1910 he signed a contract, somewhat reluctantly, with the Cincinnati club, agreeing that he should be fined twenty-five dollars every time he took a drink of liquor during the playing season. This contract apparently served its purpose and kept McLean reasonably sober, for he was not fined often.

When the time came for drawing up his 1911 contract, however, Larry announced his belief that the agreement was unilateral—that he got no appreciable benefit from it.

"I'm going to ask for a clause," he said, "under which I will be paid a quarter for each time I refuse when somebody wants to buy me a drink. I am willing to pay for the services of a guard who will stay with me day and night. All he will have to do will be to keep account of the number of times I refuse drinks which are offered to me and report the daily totals to the club management."

The club management said no.

A COUNTY JUDGE named A. H. F. Seegar once held court in the middle of the bleachers during a ball game at Middletown, New York. The date was July 25, 1910, and the Cuban Giants were playing the Middletown Athletic Club.

Judge Seegar was enjoying the contest, which had reached the fourth inning, when an attorney tapped him on the shoulder. The lawyer said he wanted to get the court's official permission to examine some grand-jury minutes in a certain case. The judge was about to denounce the lawyer for bothering him at such a time and place, when he noticed, sitting not far away, the district attorney for the county. The judge summoned the prosecutor and announced, "We'll settle this thing right now. Wait a minute." A roar from the crowd brought the judge to his feet. He surveyed the field and saw that a Middletown man had just tripled. "Attaboy!" cried the court, then resumed his seat. "Let's hear the arguments," he ordered. The two attorneys spoke their pieces with only one interruption—a run scored—and

Judge Seegar swiftly ruled that the jury minutes might be inspected. "Now," concluded His Honor, "please go away and leave me alone."

 A CLEVELAND OUTFIELDER named Moffitt encountered extraordinary difficulties when he went after a high fly ball during a game with Chicago one afternoon in 1884.

Just as Moffitt started his run, a dog came onto the field. The dog appeared to believe that Moffitt was running from him in fright and went for the outfielder. Moffitt stayed on his course despite the fact that the dog was soon nipping at his legs. In the same instant that he caught the ball the fielder kicked the dog in the head, and the dog lit out for the side lines.

Moffitt took quick stock of the situation. Nobody on base. He whirled around, cocked his arm, and threw the ball with all his might—a perfect peg it was, too, for it hit the fleeing dog squarely in the backside and knocked him essover appetite.

 IN THE EARLY YEARS of this century Herman (Germany) Schaefer, already celebrated as a comedian on the baseball diamond, acquired a different reputation. He became, in the popular mind, a baseball soothsayer—capable of calling the turn in ball games.

Apparently it all began one June day in 1912 when Schaefer's team, Washington, was playing at Chicago. Moeller had just stepped to the plate for Washington when Schaefer, coaching at first, turned around and faced the spectators. Assuming an awkward sort of stance, he announced to the crowd, "This is the way I always stand when I want a man to hit a single." On the next pitch, Moeller singled. It seems likely that the performance made as great an impression on Schaefer as it did on the fans, because he continued for a while to exercise his occult talents. Baseball writers of the period were often astounded by his accuracy. About a week after the Chicago incident Schaefer was coaching in a game against Cleveland. In the sixth inning Shanks of Washington was at bat with two strikes on him. Schaefer yelled out to the Cleveland center fielder, "Back up, you idiot! Shanks always triples over the center fielder's head when he gets two strikes on him!" The center fielder yelled back a recommendation that Schaefer go to hell. Whereupon Shanks tripled over his head. And Schaefer, so pleased with himself, turned around, assumed a new sort of posture, and told the crowd, "This is the way I always stand when I want the score to be 6 to 3 in our favor." At the end of the game that was the score.

IN 1905 the Washington club was being criticized from every direction for its poor showing in the league, and many of the fans believed that the team's nickname, Senators, was an affliction amounting to a jinx. There was a public demand that the nickname be changed, and a committee of newspapermen met to decide on a new one. They settled on Nationals—the name of an earlier club which had represented the national capital quite famously. Among the nicknames considered at the meeting were Rough Riders, Teddyites, Has Beens, and Tailenders.

ONCE UPON A TIME there was an umpire named Gaffney. He functioned in a period when a baseball game sometimes had more the aspect of warfare than of mild athletic diversion.

There was an afternoon in Philadelphia when Gaffney was at work behind the plate. In the course of a series of decisions he found that the crowd behind him was growing restive, and there were occasional shouts which indicated that certain spectators had a desire to break his—Gaffney's—neck. He went on with his work, however, and the hooting grew in intensity. Hate was heavy in the air.

Suddenly a spectator emerged from the stands, scrambled over the fence which separated the customers from the playing field, and moved upon Umpire Gaffney.

The umpire squared off, ready for battle. He was quickly able to recognize two important facts. The approaching spectator was of a mind to commit violent assault. And, point two, the approaching spectator was somewhat drunk. Umpire Gaffney had an idea.

As the belligerent fan came within a few yards of him, the umpire spoke to him in a low and confident tone.

"Mister," he said, "I sure appreciate the way you've come down here to show the rest of these crazy people that you're on my side. It's fellas like you that make an umpire feel that his work is worth while, that he's got at least a few friends in the world."

The drunk stopped, stared, shook his head briefly in an effort to clear it.

"Sure as me name's Flaherty," he said then to Gaffney, "me and you together can take the whole lot of thim on!"

76

With that he whirled around and faced the angry crowd, holding up his hands to command silence, and when he got it he yelled:

"Anybody up there that's got anything against my friend Gaffney here, let 'em state it, and they got me to deal with!"

Somehow the thing caught the fancy of the crowd and in a moment they were laughing and even cheering, and Umpire Gaffney went through the remainder of the game without a bit of abuse being thrown at him.

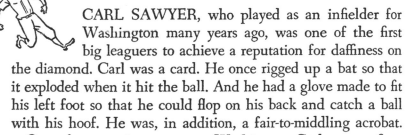

CARL SAWYER, who played as an infielder for Washington many years ago, was one of the first big leaguers to achieve a reputation for daffiness on the diamond. Carl was a card. He once rigged up a bat so that it exploded when it hit the ball. And he had a glove made to fit his left foot so that he could flop on his back and catch a ball with his hoof. He was, in addition, a fair-to-middling acrobat.

One afternoon in a game at Washington Carl got on first, and the next batter blasted the ball to left field with the hit-and-run signal on. Carl rounded second and noted that the coach at third was waving for him to keep coming. It was a bum job of coaching. The ball arrived in the third baseman's hands well ahead of the runner. It came in low, and the third baseman took it squarely on the base path, about four feet in front of the bag.

Carl Sawyer came galloping up just as the third baseman stooped to take the ball. Normally a base runner would have crashed into the man or made an effort to dodge around him. Not Carl. He threw himself into the air, turned a neat somersault, and landed with his feet on the bag.

Silk O'Loughlin, the umpire, witnessed Carl's flight with

popeyed amazement, then recovered his aplomb and cried: "Yer out!"

Carl didn't agree with the decision. He stomped and screamed and called the umpire bad names and called the umpire's mother a bad name and demanded an official explanation of why he was out. O'Loughlin gave him one.

"You left the base path," said the umpire, "and that ain't legal."

 THERE WAS ONCE a first baseman named Robert Unglaub.

Before he went to the major leagues, Unglaub played with Milwaukee and was with that club during a road trip back about 1903.

Joe Cantillon was managing Milwaukee, and one evening in Indianapolis Joe and several of his players went for a stroll in the downtown section of the Hoosier city.

They came to a corner where a Salvation Army street meeting was in progress and stood back and watched it for a while.

Suddenly a man stepped out of the Salvation Army band, removed his hat, and started talking. Joe Cantillon and his players were aghast—for it was Bob Unglaub.

Bob then and there testified before the Lord that he was an evil man with evil ways.

"I am sorry to admit it," he said, "but I am a baseball player. I don't know how I ever got into such a degrading, sinful business. It is an awful game and the men who play it are sinners, not fit for God-fearing people to associate with."

Manager Cantillon saw that his players were beginning to bristle and to mutter threateningly. Fascinated by the spectacle, he restrained them and compelled them to listen to Unglaub's

testimonial through to the end. Robert really gave baseball and baseball players holy hell.

Telling the story a few years later, Manager Cantillon was asked if Unglaub had repented and quit the game.

"Hell no," said the manager. "He was the first man in line at the pay window on the first and fifteenth of every month."

 IT IS A RARE THING to find an umpire involved in the rigging of a practical joke, yet there is one instance at least in which it happened.

The day before the Western League season was to open at Minneapolis in 1897, Frank March, who was to umpire the opener, went to the grounds keeper for the Minneapolis club. March said that he had just received word from Ban Johnson ordering that, for the opening game, the field be painted white with the foul lines black.

The grounds keeper was perplexed, of course, but Umpire March was helpful.

"Tell you what you do," he said. "Get a street-sprinkler wagon and fill it full of whitewash and use that to paint the field."

The grounds keeper started making arrangements, but soon reached the realization that the holes in the sprinkler nozzles of the city's street wagons were too small for the passage of whitewash and that they would clog up quickly. He tried to talk city officials into letting him enlarge the holes on a single wagon, but they told him to go away. At last the harried grounds keeper took his troubles to club headquarters, where in time he was tipped to the truth. Baseball records (thorough as they are) contain no account of what he did to Umpire March.

JACK POWELL, a pitcher for the St. Louis Browns in 1908, had perfect control in the clutch.

One afternoon the fans in a certain section of the bleachers were jeering Powell unmercifully. He ignored the ragging for a long time, then he got mad. He turned around and looked at the crowd and picked out the face of a man named Gleason, who seemed to be leading the hecklers. Then he let one go, high and hard, and it struck Gleason squarely in the mouth, knocking out his front teeth.

Gleason sued the pitcher, and the jury, after listening to Powell's side of the story, decided the pitcher was justified.

EVER HEAR of a pitcher named Manghbwebeke, who had a good curve ball?

Here is a letter that came many years ago out of Dahomey, Africa. It was written by Arthur Duggan, who had once been a professional baseball pitcher in Chicago. Says Duggan:

> There are baseball teams of men at Savalou, at Nikki, and at Dunkassa that can put up a fair article of baseball, but the women are stronger and more agile and they like the game better. I don't know where they learned the game. Possibly they caught onto it from some of their fellow natives who were sold into slavery in the United States and

later returned to their homeland. At any rate they play with three bases, set in a triangle, with the pitcher in the center. The number of outfielders is limited only by the number of those who wish to play.

The balls are made of fiber from a tree. They are covered with monkey skin or lion skin. The bats are of wood and slightly flattened.

Wilson, a civil engineer from Elmira, New York, took one team in hand and I handled another club. Wilson's team was all-male; mine was composed entirely of women. When we clashed in our first game, my Amazons won by a score of 47 to 23. The spectators sat on a hillside.

Later on Wilson, seeing that the women played a better game than the men, organized an all-female club to do battle with my team. Both Wilson and I agreed not to play with our teams, as we had in the first game.

I started right away to develop one of the native girls as a pitcher to take my place on the team. Her name is Manghbwebeke, as near as I can figure it out. We called her Belle. She has learned how to throw a curve ball.

 BALLPLAYERS, as a rule, try to keep their emotions in leash when they are traded or sold against their wishes. Germany Schaefer, the great and goofy infielder, was a notable exception. In the time when he was a minor leaguer, playing with St. Paul, he was notified just before the start of a game that he had been traded to Milwaukee and that on this, his last day, he would be assigned to coach at first base. He accepted the assignment, but not graciously. All through the game he displayed his unhappiness by shrieking madly, leaping up and down, hurling his cap to the ground, running around in circles, and several times falling to the turf and madly eating grass.

BASEBALL was recognized as the national pastime in the Mardi Gras celebration at New Orleans back in the early 1880s. A large float served as a representation of the game and featured a huge baseball being struck by a bat. The players surrounded this centerpiece and were caricatured with enormous bumps on their heads, blackened eyes, and assorted bandages with the bloodstains showing through. The spectators were represented by frogs and marsh hens.

ONE OF the most splendiferous editorial bouquets ever tossed into the lap of the national pastime appeared back in 1909 in the *Saturday Evening Post* and was widely reprinted by the daily press. It follows:

> It is important to remember, in an imperfect and fretful world, that we have one institution which is practically above reproach and above

criticism. Nobody worth mentioning wants to change its constitution or limit its powers. The government is not asked to inspect, regulate, suppress, guarantee, or own it.

There is no movement afoot that we know of to uplift it, like the stage, or to abolish it, like marriage. No one complains that it is vulgar, like the newspapers, or that it assassinates genius, like the magazines. It rouses no class passions and, while it has magnates, they go unhung, with our approval.

This one comparatively perfect flower of our sadly defective civilization is—of course—baseball, the only important institution, so far as we can remember, which the United States regards with a practically universal approval.

ARLIE LATHAM contributed some lively moments to an otherwise dull game one afternoon in St. Louis. Arlie had been coaching at first base all afternoon, comporting himself with unaccustomed dignity. In the seventh inning, with nobody on base and nothing unusual happening on the field, Arlie suddenly began signaling frantically to the umpire to call time. The umpire was puzzled, but complied. Thereupon Mr. Latham appeared to embark upon a lively epileptic fit. He began running around in circles. Then he'd stop and stomp his feet furiously on the ground. After that he'd race across the diamond, and once ran almost to the outfield bleachers, where he stopped to paw the ground, then dashed back. The impression was growing that the great Arlie

Latham had suddenly gone mad. For a while everyone simply watched him in amazement. Then, when he appeared to be returning to the coaching box, players and officials and policemen swarmed around him.

"What's the matter?" they cried. "What happened?"

"Oh, nothing," said Arlie. "My feet just went to sleep."

A NEAT DOUBLE PLAY was executed forty years or so ago by a pitcher's slab in Denver.

St. Joseph was playing at Denver. The city had been suffering from a long, dry spell and the pitcher's mound, lacking moisture, had been crumbling away all afternoon beneath the pivoting feet of the hurlers. Consequently the rubber slab was deeply exposed in the direction of home plate.

Denver was batting in the seventh, trailing by a couple of runs. The home team got the bases loaded, and the next man slashed the ball directly at the pitcher's feet. It looked like a sure thing to shoot over second and into center field. Instead it struck the slab and came sailing back toward the plate. The St. Joe catcher collected his wits quickly, grabbed the ball from the air, stepped on home, and then fired down to first to get the runner. Accounts of the freak play make mention of the fact that the runner, upon realizing what had happened, used language that would have shocked a mule.

MANAGER BILLY VOLTZ of Chattanooga had a problem one afternoon in 1885 when his right fielder took sick during a game with the Macon,

Georgia, team. Voltz had no one to send in as replacement except a utility catcher named Bullas.

This Bullas was a fairly expert performer back of the plate but in right field he seemed to be out of his element. Fortunately for Chattanooga, however, the Macon batsmen hit few balls to right field—that is, until the ninth inning. Then things got really "crooshial."

Macon, trailing by a single run, managed to get men on second and third. Two out. The next batter laced a long fly to right.

Mr. Bullas, the misplaced catcher, probably was the only man in the park who was not certain about where that ball was headed. He started toward the infield. Then he realized that he should be traveling toward the fence. He turned around and dug for the depths of right field until he reached a point where he felt the time had come for him to look up and get some idea as to the whereabouts of that ball. He looked up, only to be blinded by the late-afternoon sun. He couldn't find the ball, but the ball found him. It hit him on the top of his head, and, one or the other being resilient, bounced in a graceful arc across the top of the fence for a game-winning homer.

CAP ANSON, one of baseball's greatest hitters, was also one of the game's greatest fanatics when it came to bats. The Cincinnati *Enquirer* reported in 1897:

> There are more loose timbers around the Chicago ball park and Spalding's store than it would take to start a good-sized lumberyard. In

odd nooks and corners at the ball yard especially you will run onto an old log, a wagon tongue, or an old cart shaft.

Anson has either taken them there himself or has had them hauled in. They are timber for his bats. He never overlooks a good piece of wood, no matter where he is.

If he sees a well-seasoned and solid piece of wood in Galveston, New York, or San Francisco, he will ship it to Chicago. Someday, when he thinks of it again, he will haul it out and have it turned into a bat.

It has been stated that he has two hundred and seventy-six bats in the basement of his home but there are some who say the figure is closer to five hundred. He has them hung up like hams. His locker is always full of bats. He never permits anybody else to use any stick in his private stock.

MATTY FITZGERALD started his umpiring career as a young man in the days when the umpire normally stationed himself behind the pitcher.

He was officiating one afternoon at a contest between the Logan Squares and the Gunthers—two semi-pro teams in Chicago. Between innings Matty slipped a supply of extra baseballs inside his shirt, then took his place behind the pitcher.

As the pitcher began a windup, Matty bent forward to watch the pitch. One of the spare balls dropped from his shirt just as the pitcher cut loose. The batter hit a screaming grounder back toward the box, and the batted ball struck the ball that had dropped near the umpire's feet.

One ball shot off toward the shortstop, the other bobbed along to the second baseman. Both infielders threw to first. Frank McNichols, the first baseman, reached his left hand high and caught the shortstop's throw; with his right hand he grabbed the throw from second.

There could have been a ticklish question, but there wasn't.

"Yer out!" cried Matty. "Both balls beat you to the sack!"

CHRIS VON DER AHE, fabulous president of the St. Louis Browns in the 1880s, walked into the clubhouse one day and discovered that some of the equipment had been badly damaged.

Chris summoned the members of the team and then demanded to know who had been damaging the property. No one answered. Chris surveyed the scene a moment, then announced, "I'll give one hundred dollars to find out who did it." Another long silence, during which Arlie Latham, the team's third baseman, pondered the possibilities. Finally Arlie spoke.

"I know who done it."

"Who?"

"Give me the hundred dollars first," Arlie insisted.

The money was handed over.

"I did it," said Latham.

Whereupon Chris let out a roar.

"For that," he yelled, "I'm fining you fifty dollars!"

Then he stomped out of the room, bristling, satisfied that nobody could get away with anything on Old Chris.

LEAPING DAVE ALTIZER, a talented short-stop for the old Chicago White Sox, amused himself sometimes with little practical jokes, using his teammates as victims. It was inevitable that someday his sins would catch up with him.

One afternoon the White Sox were playing Cleveland. Dave got a base on balls. On the next pitch he lowered his head and started for second. He heard the crack of the bat against the ball, but he didn't look to see what happened. Actually the ball had been lined straight at the first baseman, who had then touched first for the double play.

Nick Altrock was coaching at third and saw that both the batter and Dave had been put out. He saw quickly, too, that Dave didn't know what had happened, so Nick yelled:

"Slide, Dave! Slide!"

And Dave slid into second.

At this point the Cleveland first baseman got into the spirit of things. Just as Dave raised his head and looked around, the first baseman heaved the ball wildly into left field. And over near third Nick Altrock was howling for Dave to get off the ground and head for third. Dave did. He charged down the line and went into a magnificent slide as the ball, intentionally thrown high by the left fielder, shot over the base and rolled toward the stands.

Once more Dave got to his feet and once more started running. The catcher had the ball as Dave went into another awesome slide, but the catcher purposely missed the tag by a mile.

"You're out!" cried the umpire.

Leaping to his feet, Dave screamed a protest.

"You blind son of a bitch!" he roared at the umpire. "He missed me by two feet!"

"You dumb son of a bitch!" responded the umpire. "You were out at first base!"

Ever afterward Dave Altizer seemed to carry a grudge against umpires and on one occasion, at least, his belligerence proved quite embarrassing. He was at bat, and the count went to three balls and two strikes. Dave let the next pitch, a sweeping curve, go past him and heard the umpire call it strike three. He whirled around and started shrieking. He was so preoccupied with the job of cussing that he failed to note that the ball had been missed by the catcher and had gone back to the stands. Had he known it, he would have had ample time to get to third, but he stood there howling obscenities. Meanwhile his teammates were screaming for him to run to first, but Dave thought they were only supporting him in his verbal assault on the umpire and renewed the profane attack with fresh vigor. All of which gave the third baseman a chance to retrieve the ball and toss it to first for the put-out.

A COUPLE of years ago Peter Arno did a cartoon for *The New Yorker* showing a section of the grandstand at a ball park. The fans in the picture were all in a high sweat of anger. In the center stood a minister of the gospel, his face contorted with fury, and he was crying out, "Thou hath eyes to see and see not!"

Of all the taunts that come the way of the umpire, the charge of defective eyesight is probably the most common. At least once in baseball history the authorities took some cognizance of it.

In 1911 Thomas J. Lynch, president of the National League and himself a former umpire, grew weary of the eternal shouts from the stands reflecting on the vision of the league's umpires. He ordered that all members of the league umpiring staff undergo thorough eye tests.

When the reports of the various oculists were in, they were turned over to Dr. Royal S. Copeland, a former professor of ophthalmology who would later become a United States senator. Dr. Copeland studied them and then submitted his own report. The lowest score made by any one umpire was "normal vision," while most of them had better-than-average eyesight and a few had vision that was remarkably acute.

FOR LACK of a ball a game was lost.

This story dates back to 1895 and concerns one of the most bizarre home runs ever belted.

Rochester was playing at Springfield, Massachusetts, on a June afternoon that year. Springfield had a commanding lead when the game reached the seventh inning. O'Brien, the Rochester third baseman, took his place at the plate and walloped the ball high and far. When it came down it hit water, dropping into the river that flowed past the outfield. It was a homer and scored a run, but Rochester was still half-a-dozen runs behind. Yet O'Brien's clout really won the game for his team.

In the eighth inning one of the Springfield players met the ball squarely, and it broke in half.

The rules said that the home team was required to furnish the baseballs, and now Umpire Gaffney called upon the Springfield bench to toss out another ball. Nothing happened. The Springfield men simply didn't have another ball. They had started with two. One went into the river. The second was split in half. There was much scurrying about and searching, but nary a ball could be found in the park. Finally Umpire Gaffney

announced with some disgust that he was forfeiting the game
to Rochester, and it went into the books as a Rochester victory.

THE INSTITUTION known as Ladies' Day at
the ball parks is almost as old as bats.
During the season of 1897 in Washington one
day each week was designated as Ladies' Day, meaning that
females did not have to pay admission that afternoon. It happened in that season that hordes of females turned out for certain games which were not free—where they had to pay just the
same as the men. The reason lay in the person of one Winnie
Mercer, a Washington pitcher.

Winnie Mercer had become a sort of matinee idol. The
women were just wild about Winnie. When word got around
that he was to pitch, the petticoats sometimes outnumbered the
britches in the stands.

We come now to an afternoon in September with Winnie
Mercer on the mound and the stands awash with women.
These women behaved that day as many other women would
behave years later at the mere thought of Rudolph Valentino
and as teen-age girls of the early 1940s would behave upon
hearing the voice of Frank Sinatra.

The umpire was a gentleman named Carpenter. There is a
faint suggestion in contemporary accounts of the game that Mr.
Carpenter was either jealous of Winnie Mercer or contemptuous of him because of the adoration of the whinnying herd. Be
that as it may, the handsome pitcher began showing signs of
dissatisfaction with the manner in which Carpenter was calling
the balls and strikes.

The stands, to a woman, sided with Winnie, of course. Then
came an incident along about the fifth inning which really pro-

voked the Winnie-worshipers. On his way from the bench to the mound Winnie walked up to Umpire Carpenter and handed him a pair of eyeglasses. The ladies shrieked with delight. But Umpire Carpenter was not amused. He handed the glasses back to Winnie and then expelled Winnie from the game for conduct unbecoming a horse's behind.

Oh, the nerve of him! Oh, what a beast! The ladies screeched and howled in a jungle chorus. All the fury that they usually hoarded for the Christmas shopping rush boiled out of them, aimed at poor Umpire Carpenter. But he ignored it, or pretended to ignore it, and the game went along without the presence of Hero Winnie.

The passion of the females never subsided after that, but seemed to grow more intense and ominous with each inning. Then along toward the end of the game there was a close play on the base paths, and Umpire Carpenter called it against the home team, wiping out any chance that Washington might have had to win. Now the ladies really let him have it, and it is said that some of them used language that would have got them thrown out of any Grade-B bordello.

As the last out was made, hundreds of infuriated females crowded past the front rows of seats, shouting threatening things at poor Carpenter, and the benighted umpire, who never quailed before the fury of a male mob, hastened to cover. He made a dash for the business office of the Washington ball club behind the stands . . . and the admirers of Winnie Mercer pursued him.

Once inside the office Umpire Carpenter called upon the staff members to help protect him, and they went to work closing the heavy shutters, because already a few stones and bricks were beginning to crash against the structure, and one window had been broken.

The ladies used their parasols to beat against the shutters, and some found clubs which they employed against the door, all the while screaming what they were going to do to Carpenter once they got their hands on his filthy hide. The mob grew in numbers as time went on, and several female platoons armed with clubs were sent to guard the main exit against the chance that Carpenter would try to sneak out that way.

Meanwhile somebody in the office figured out a way of escape. Carpenter was taken through a rear door and made his way beneath the stands, where at times he had to crawl, to a side entrance of the park. There a team of fast horses awaited him, and whirled him off to . . . well, he probably asked that he be taken to Alaska.

The female mob hung on for an hour after that, doing some damage to the administration building; then it began to get dark, and the ladies slowly dispersed, returning to their homes to jounce and google their little children and, no doubt, abuse their husbands. This latter is a mere speculative observation. We have no concrete facts to support it.

THE NEW YORK *Clipper* in 1886 carried a report on the injury of Johnny Hogan, center fielder for the Atlanta team, in a game with Nashville. The headline called it "A Singular Accident," and Mr. Hogan, when he felt like talking, said he was glad it wasn't plural.

Early in the game Billy Taylor of Nashville caught hold of a ball and belted it toward the center-field fence. Hogan promptly turned his back and started running. As he neared the fence he glanced back to see how he was doing. Just then his foot went into a shallow drain ditch near the base of the fence, and Hogan crashed into the boards head first, the way a fullback rams his way into a line.

When the top of Hogan's head struck the fence there was a splintering crash; his head had driven a neat hole right through the boards, and there he hung. Everyone in the park figured he had broken both his skull and his neck. He was withdrawn from the aperture and stretched on the ground, and in a little while he got up and started rubbing his scalp and twisting his head this way and that to test his neck bones. A doctor soon ascertained that he was not seriously hurt, and after he was patched up and had a little rest he resumed playing.

ASSIGNED to the job of scorekeeper in a game at Morristown, Ohio, one day in 1902, a young man named Stanton Walker found that his pencil needed sharpening in one of the late innings. He asked the man sitting next to him for a knife. Walker had just started to put a new point on his pencil when a hard foul ball shot back of the plate, struck his hand, and drove the blade of the knife into his heart.

AS OWNER of the St. Louis Browns, the incomparable Chris Von der Ahe was always seriously concerned over the conduct of his team as well as its individual members. Chris was born in Germany and spoke with a heavy accent.

After every game Chris and other members of the Browns' "high command" would hold a meeting and discuss the individual performances and decide on which players needed to be scolded. During these executive sessions a man named Muckenfuss, who was secretary of the club, took notes. Then it was his job to write out a speech for President Von der Ahe—a speech embodying all the points to be delivered the next day when the team was assembled.

Old-timers say there was nothing funnier than those speeches. Secretary Muckenfuss was a man of humor, and in composing the scripts for Von der Ahe rendered them as complex as possible and scattered big words through them. The players themselves had the tough assignments—it being required of them through agreement that they should control themselves and never laugh until after the meetings were over.

 THE MASK worn by umpires behind the plate was introduced for the primary purpose of protecting the official's face from foul tips; it also has served an important secondary purpose—that of protecting the face from fists.

In the days when physical combat was more general in ball games the mask was often used as a weapon. Many an umpire has taken off his mask during combat, seized it by the straps, and used it to flog the enemy on the head.

A piece of business involving the umpire's mask precipitated one of the wildest afternoons ever seen on a baseball diamond in Buffalo. The Buffalo shortstop, named Nattress, was banished from the game by Umpire Hassett after the player had addressed "a most evil remark" to the umpire. Nattress in a fury rushed up to the official, took hold of his mask, pulled it out as far as the elastic straps would permit, then let it snap back onto Hassett's face. The free-for-all that followed ended with Umpire Hassett forfeiting the game to Buffalo.

Bull Perrine was an umpire in the Pacific Coast League before moving on to the majors. One day he was umpiring a game between Oakland and San Francisco. The San Francisco catcher spent most of the afternoons criticizing Perrine's decisions and making most evil remarks to him. Perrine, in turn, gave the catcher the rough side of his tongue and at last the catcher lost his temper.

"If you would take off that mask," he said, "I'd sure slam you one on the jaw."

"Oh, you would, would you?" said Perrine, taking off the mask.

The catcher slammed him one on the jaw. Perrine regained consciousness two hours later, and his first words, when he was able to talk, were, "What a fool I was to take off that mask!"

ARLIE LATHAM was not only a great clown on the diamond but he could rise to impressive dramatic heights when the occasion demanded.

Back in the 1880s, during a game with Baltimore, Arlie was playing third base for the St. Louis Browns. Baltimore was at bat in the last of the ninth, and St. Louis was ahead 6 to 5. Baltimore managed to get a runner on third, and the St. Louis pitcher snapped the ball over to Latham in an attempt to catch the runner off the bag. But the runner cleverly flipped his elbow beneath Latham's arm, causing Arlie to miss the ball entirely and permitting the runner to score and tie up the game.

Arlie howled in anger and carried his case to the umpire, but he was overruled. The umpire announced that the run counted. Whereupon Arlie turned and faced the spectators in the grandstand and delivered the following oration:

"Ladies and gentlemen, after what has just happened I want to say that when this game comes to an end I will never again take part in the game of baseball. I am through forever . . .

through with a sport that permits this kind of highway robbery."

The game was resumed, went on to the twelfth inning, and in that inning St. Louis won it.

On the following day Arlie Latham was, as usual, at third base.

AUGUST the twenty-second, 1885, was a bad day to do any business in the community of Lawrence, Kansas.

On the day before there had been a baseball game, staged to raise funds for a monument honoring Ulysses S. Grant.

One team was composed of county officials and the other of local businessmen. The players ranged in age from forty to seventy.

The registrar of deeds was running out a two-base hit when he fell and broke his arm.

The county clerk broke his shoulder.

A deputy sheriff got several teeth knocked down his throat by a batted ball.

A prominent grocer dislocated his knee.

A druggist broke two fingers.

The county officials won, 51 to 41.

The take at the gate was $150.

The doctors' bills came to $180.

THE LOYALTY of baseball fans cannot be properly discussed without mention of one S. D. Reed. An American League contest was being played in

Detroit early in 1905, and the game, a squeaker, had gone into the eleventh inning.

Suddenly Umpire Jack Sheridan turned toward the grandstand, raised his hand to command silence, and announced, "Is S. D. Reed in the stands? He is wanted at home. His house is on fire."

There was a small commotion back of first base where S. D. Reed was sitting. "Certainly," he announced loudly, "I'm S. D. Reed. But I'm not leaving. I couldn't get there in time to do anything about it. Let the damn house burn."

AN OUTFIELDER named McCreary played heads-up baseball for Louisville on an afternoon in 1895, refusing to be distracted by unusual happenings at home plate, with the result that his team tied Cincinnati.

McCreary was on base when his teammate, Second Baseman O'Brien, tried to score from third. The throw to the plate was high and the ball barely touched the tips of Catcher Vaughn's fingers as he leaped for it. Just as the Cincinnati catcher leaped high in the air, O'Brien came charging in to the plate standing up. His head struck Vaughn in the stomach, and the catcher turned a somersault. O'Brien fell to the ground, and Vaughn landed on top of him, his spikes slashing the runner's legs. The two players came off the ground fighting, and in a moment other players joined in the battle.

Meanwhile two men kept their heads. One was Umpire Keefe, who observed that O'Brien actually had touched the plate, scoring a run. The other was the aforementioned McCreary. While most of the other players were swinging fists, McCreary chugged around the bases, came down the third base line through a mob of battling ballplayers, located the plate in all that mess, touched it delicately with his toe, and tied up the game for dear old Louisville.

 ALONG ABOUT 1896 the Boston ball park had a left-field fence built along the base of a railroad embankment. In some places the boards had worked loose from the ground, leaving apertures.

On an afternoon when Boston was playing Chicago, the Boston left fielder was Billy Hamilton, who knew that tricky left-field fence like a brother. Billy was playing in fairly close when a Chicago batter sent a fly over his head. Billy went after it and saw it roll beneath the fence. Rushing up to the boards, he dropped to his knees and reached through the hole where the ball had disappeared. All he felt was a tin can. He quickly pulled the can through the hole and saw that the ball was inside it. He shook it vigorously, but the ball was stuck in the can. He quickly tried to dig it out with his fingers, but he couldn't get hold of it. Looking up, he saw the runner had reached third and was steaming for home. Billy threw the can to an infielder, who took one startled look at what had landed in his glove, then relayed the whole mess to the catcher. And the catcher got it just in time to slap it against the runner as he came sliding into the plate. "Yer out!" cried the umpire, and the decision stood in spite of an avalanche of protests—the main contention being, of course, that the ball had never actually touched the runner.

That ball-in-the-can incident would appear to be without parallel in the history of baseball, before or after, yet the play had its counterpart in the same decade and in the same city. There was one major difference—the umpire's decision.

This time Cleveland was playing at Boston. A ball was

knocked into the outfield where it rolled into a tomato can that somehow had got onto the field. Outfielder Hughie Duffy saw the ball go into the can. He didn't fool with it at all. He picked up the can and let go a spiral pass all the way to home plate, where the catcher tagged the runner with the canned ball. "Safe!" yelled the umpire. And when the inevitable howls arose, the official said simply, "They's nothin' in the rule book that says you can put out a runner by touchin' him with a tomater can."

 ONE OF the most remarkable bats ever used in baseball came out of Ohio.

Around 1880 the old Ohio State Penitentiary was being razed, and a rising young ballplayer named Perring happened to be present on the day the prison scaffold was coming down. The platform had been used in the hanging of dozens of criminals. Perring was attracted by the quality of the hickory wood that had gone into its construction. In common with many other old-time ballplayers, Perring was always on the prowl for new bats. He acquired one of the heavy beams from the scaffold and had a bat made from it. He used that bat for twenty years, right up to the day he retired from baseball, and then he handed it over to his son George Perring. George got it in 1906 and always cherished the old piece of gallows wood, which he used in establishing a fine hitting record for himself, notably with Kansas City in the old Federal League. Writing about the bat in 1910, a sports writer said:

"George permits no one else to touch his bat, much less take it up to the plate. He carries it to and from the park in a special case. The timber from which the hangman's rope dangled in the long ago has been punishing the pitchs during more than thirty years."

 CATCHERS' MASKS were just beginning to come into general use in the 1880s. Protective equipment had for a long time been scorned by the he-men of the diamond, but now the value of the mask was being recognized, even though the early "bird cages," as they were called, were actually a danger in themselves. Fashioned of comparatively light materials, foul tips sometimes drove pieces of wire into the faces they were supposed to protect.

One day in 1884, when Detroit and Boston were playing, Catcher Mike Hines of the Red Sox raised his hands too late to stop a foul tip. The ball struck his mask. In this instance the wires didn't break—they just spread enough to hold the ball in a tight grip. Hines was trying to wrestle the ball loose when a ruckus arose around him. Umpire Van Court had called the batter out. Detroit players swarmed about him, protesting the decision. But Van Court would not change his ruling—Hines, he said, had caught the foul tip on the third strike.

 IT MAY have happened in Pittsburgh or Salt Lake City or Boston or Birmingham. Surely it *has* happened at one time or another in baseball history.

A batter stands at the plate with two strikes on him. The ball comes steaming in.

"Strike three!" cries the umpire.

"Wait a minute!" protests the batter. "That wasn't over the plate."

"Oh, it wasn't?" says the umpire, surprised. "Okay. Ball two!"

SAM LEEVER, who used to pitch for Pittsburgh, was listed among the holdouts every spring.

At the appropriate time the Pittsburgh club would mail a contract to Sam at his home. Then the long wait, with no word from the pitcher. Finally President Barney Dreyfuss would address an envelope to Sam and enclose nothing but a two-cent stamp in it. And when the stamp arrived at Sam's home he'd mail back his signed contract.

IT WAS really hot that day in Columbus back in the 1890s, and Ralph Johnson, playing left field, wasn't enjoying it. The thermometer registered above one hundred, and the sun was blazing down on the field. Finally Johnson moved from his customary position so he could stand in the shade thrown by the high outfield fence.

Almost at once Manager Al Buckenburger, sitting on the bench, was on his feet. He yelled out to Jack O'Connor, the field captain, "Tell Johnson to get back in position!" The captain relayed the message, but Johnson refused to come out of the shade. Captain O'Connor called time and walked out to the fence and had a talk with the left fielder. After that Johnson emerged into the sunlight—but not for long. Gradually, while playing his position, he eased back until he was once again in the shade. Whereupon Manager Buckenburger, rushing halfway out to the fence, yelled:

"I'm fining you twenty-five dollars for that! Get the hell back to your position and remember this: every time you hit that shade it's another twenty-five!"

Thereafter Johnson occupied his place in the sun.

THERE'S A MORAL for the young in this little story, for which the authors apologize. It can't be helped.

In 1906 a boy named Matthew Ritter, age thirteen, wanted desperately to watch a baseball game in his home town of Jeffersonville, Indiana. Matthew climbed a big oak tree outside the park and perched himself on a limb where he could see the contest. In one of the late innings a Jeffersonville man walloped a three-base hit. Matthew released his hold on the limb to cup his hands at his mouth and yell. He fell, and when he hit the ground bit off his own tongue.

REGARDLESS of all evidence to the contrary, umpires are human beings. There have been, among their numbers, many rugged individualists. Bill Byron, for example. He was known as "The Humming-bird" for the reason that he always burst into song whenever a player protested one of his decisions.

Jack Sheridan, a colorful American League umpire back in the early years of the century, often had to fight his way out of the park after a ball game. One day a sports writer encountered Sheridan in a hotel lobby and noticed that the umpire appeared to be unhappy. The writer asked him what had happened.

"Lost my pocketknife," said Sheridan. "You know—that long one of mine. Carried it twenty-five years, and it got me out of many a tough spot. All I had to do was whip 'er out, flick open the long blade, and they cleared a path for me."

Sheridan was famous for another reason. He was one of the original boosters for California. It was his custom to get in a plug for his home town on the West coast whenever he found the slightest opportunity. For a long time he made a practice of throwing in an ad for the town whenever a batter let a third strike go by. If the ball came zipping across the plate and the batter failed to swing at it, Sheridan would cry magnificently:

"Strike three! San José, California! The Garden Spot of America!"

WHEN THE old-time hot-stove leagues got to steaming, someone usually came up with the story about a ball game that was played one day in Memphis. One of the baseball characters in Memphis was a spectator who fancied himself as a great authority on the game and who was always begging for an opportunity to umpire a game.

So one afternoon he was given that chance, and he did quite well back of the plate until about the fifth inning. A team from Atlanta was at bat with one out when a slugger belted one high and far into the outfield.

The outfielder for the visiting team ran like a jackrabbit, made a spectacular over-the-shoulder catch, fell down, turned over two or three times, and came up with the ball clutched in his hand.

The umpire's eyes bugged out as he saw this sensational fielding performance. He hesitated a moment, then shouted his decision.

"Batter's out!" he yelled. "An' the side's out. That ketch was twice as good as any ketch I ever seen, so it's good for two outs steader one!"

 A NEW YORK *Clipper* item in 1883 told of an umpire in West Philadelphia who had a singular way of calling strikes. He always referred to a strike as a "plunge." Whenever a batter struck out, the umpire would deliver a summarization of the count so all could hear, as follows:

"One plunge, two plunges, three plunges, and the plunger is out!"

A DRAMATIC ninth-inning home run was the deciding factor in a game in 1898 at St. Paul.

On a Sunday afternoon the St. Paul club was playing Minneapolis. Entering the ninth, St. Paul had a two-run lead behind the expert pitching of Frank Isbell, who was later to become a star infielder for the Chicago White Sox.

Minneapolis was making a valiant last-ditch stand, however, and had two men on base with two out. Isbell delivered
his pitch, the batter met it squarely, and it soared out toward
center field.

An exceptionally high wooden fence bordered the short
outfield, and the fielders had to play many fly balls as they
bounced off the boards. It was obvious that this particular fly
was going to hit high on the fence, and the St. Paul fielder
got into position so he could take it on the rebound. Back at
the plate the catcher whipped off his mask and prepared to
take the throw.

Then everybody—players as well as umpires—just waited.
The ball didn't bounce off the fence. It hit high on the boards
and stayed there, and three Minneapolis runs crossed the plate.

That ball had hit squarely on the point of a long nail that
had been driven through the boards from the other side. Eventually it had to be fielded with a ladder.

ARLIE LATHAM, third baseman for the St.
Louis Browns in the 1880s, was widely celebrated
for his clowning activities. One of his capers cost
his team the championship in 1889.

St. Louis and Brooklyn had come down the home stretch
neck and neck and were engaged in a game which would decide the championship. The contest reached the seventh inning
with St. Louis ahead, 4 to 2. At this point black clouds moved
over the field, and the St. Louis players set up a clamor to have
the game called on account of darkness. The umpire ordered
play to continue.

Arlie Latham decided to try forcing the issue. He sent the
bat boy out of the park to buy a dozen large candles. When

the boy returned, Arlie lined the candles up along the front of the St. Louis bench and then lit them. This ungentle hint had no effect on the umpire other than to cause him to walk over and blow out the flames. The moment he resumed his post back of the plate, however, Arlie scrambled out and relighted the candles. Whereupon the umpire whirled around, squared his shoulders, and announced that the game was forfeited to Brooklyn—and Brooklyn became the league champion.

IN 1909 the Rev. Father John A. Tracy, pastor of the Church of Our Lady of Good Counsel in St. Louis, received notice from his archbishop that he was being transferred to a church in Byrnesville, Missouri—a community with a population of one hundred and fifty and situated two miles from a railroad.

Father Tracy in turn notified the archbishop that he did not want to leave St. Louis and rather than take the Byrnesville assignment he would retire from active duty.

Pressed for an explanation of this decision, Father Tracy said that he had been a rooter for the St. Louis Browns for so many years that he simply couldn't face the prospect of moving to a place where it would be virtually impossible for him to attend their games.

ROWDYISM was the chief complaint made against baseball in the beginning years of the century. Then in 1909 up stepped Mrs. Frank L. Chance, wife of the Chicago Cubs' manager, with a recommendation. The women of America, she said, should flock to the ball parks—that would bring an end to the rowdyism. Mrs. Chance said further:

"If more women would forsake their bridge whist and pink tea, sofa cushions and kimonos, and turn out to watch the cleanest sport in the world, there would be more robustness and fair-mindedness among our sex.

"If women would only come out and expand their lungs by rooting for the home team, there would be less work for the doctors."

OPENING-DAY festivities in our own day appear to be fairly drab alongside the fancy-schmancy doings of the 1900s. Witness the New York *Herald's* account of the opening game at the Polo Grounds in 1905:

> All seven ages of man turned out at the Polo Grounds to make historical the opening of the baseball season of 1905 and to welcome home the champion Giants and their huge blue-and-gold streamer of bunting that proclaims the measure of Mc-Graw's merry men.
>
> To the well-timed crashing of a 21-gun salute by Captain Louis Wendell's battery, the strains of the national anthem, and the acclaim of close to 40,000 citizens of the great and enduring democracy of baseball, the Giants heaved at the long rope that sent the trailing banner swinging aloft above the grandstand.

The game was scheduled for four o'clock. At noon, when the gates were opened, humanity sprayed over the seats like water from a garden hose. By two o'clock not a seat was to be had. Sportsmen are long-suffering and kindly souls, and there is no more forgiving and indulgent a multitude than a great baseball crowd. Men clung to every vantage point, some clutching like so many bats to the rafters of the grandstand and others digging their heels into the sod banked up against the entrance promenade.

The boxes were gorgeous with pretty women. Down on the field a great horseshoe of humanity stood and bawled itself hoarse to the snarl of horns and the toot of whistles.

Right under the shadow of the great stand, bristling with flags snapping in the wind, the Seventh Regiment band discoursed the melodies of the hour.

Novelty was the trade-mark of this year's opening, and it came in the form of an automobile procession to the grounds which brought the rooters to their feet.

Peanuts and lemonade were about running out, and the great waiting crowd was becoming restive, when the northern carriage gate swung open and a series of three or four snorting, shrieking things flashed into view. Instantly the crowd was on its feet, hats swinging and shouts rising, for its idols had come at last.

Slowly the automobiles rolled along the foul lines and swung around broadside to the grandstand, honorably bearing the heaven-born.

In the first machine sat Fred. M. Knowles, secretary of the club, beaming proudly, in his new spring suit. Just behind bowled a large automobile carrying Harry Pulliam, president of the National League, and John T. Brush, president of the New York club, beaming from under a new and weirdly beautiful automobile cap.

Next came the members of the Boston team in their sorry uniforms of gray and red. Then behind them came the Giants themselves, all laundered and spotless.

All hands shelled out of the go-devils like peas out of a pod. The pennant was raised, and then a big floral horseshoe was presented to the Giants. Carrier pigeons were released and after wheeling over the diamond soared away. Then the gong clanged to announce the beginning of practice, and the work of the day was under way.

The Giants, flawless and catlike, flashed around like so much vagabond electricity as they took their practice. Easy and brilliant in every move, they made a splendid impression. John McGraw, busy as a hornet, stung them on to the swiftest kind of dashing work.

Then Johnstone, the singing umpire, made his polite announcements of the batteries and looked up expectantly to the middle box in the upper tier.

Arose then Mayor McClellan, who

flung the ball out upon the field to
the cheers of the mob. Johnstone
called, "Play ball!" and the season
was on with a vengeance.

JUST for the record, at least two umpires have
been killed by ballplayers who, infuriated over
decisions, have attacked the officials with bats.

In 1899 at Lowndesborough, Alabama, Umpire Samuel
White was killed by a player who had been abusing him all
afternoon. Umpire White, after taking the abuse for several
innings, knocked the player down; when he got up he had a bat
in his hand and used it to fracture White's skull, killing him
instantly.

Two years later, at Farmersburg, Indiana, Umpire Ora Jennings was killed in much the same way.

CHARLIE FULMER, with St. Louis in 1884, may
not have been the best ballplayer on earth, but he
was a man of distinction in another direction. He
often boasted that he was the fastest dresser in the business.
One day he made a bet with some of his teammates that he
could leave the rotunda floor of the Lindell Hotel, go to his
room on the fourth floor, and return to the rotunda in his playing clothes in four minutes. He made it with seconds to spare
and promptly issued a challenge, backed by money, that he
could dress faster than Harbridge, a member of the Cincinnati

Unions, who also had a reputation as a man who could throw on his clothes in a hurry. If Harbridge ever accepted the challenge, the records fail to show it.

AN EDITORIAL WRITER for the Chicago *Evening Post* had a severe attack of thinking one day in 1897 and proposed, in all seriousness, that the National League use women for umpires in the future.

It would tidy up the game, said the editorialist. It would do away with the vile talk so common on the playing field and the physical assaults on umpires. Baseball players would be compelled to comport themselves as gentlemen rather than roughnecks.

This proposal met with universal laughter among baseball people, yet within eight years a dame was umpiring baseball, and successfully.

Her name was Amanda Clement, and her home was at Hudson, South Dakota. Mandy had gone to college and had played baseball occasionally with the boys. Early in 1905 she talked her way into the job of umpiring professional games between teams in northwestern Iowa and South Dakota.

Mandy was described as a girl possessing "enormous personal charms," so the question of romance often entered into discussions of her professional career. Newspapermen traveled all the way from the East to watch her in action and talk with her.

"I am wedded to baseball," she said one day when someone asked her about the husky young catcher who was trying to win her heart. "I've received sixty offers of marriage from men in our league alone. But I believe I can do more good for the game and the nation by uplifting the characters of professional players who do not know how to behave."

After a couple of years of umpiring, during which she became nationally famous, Amanda abandoned baseball, went back to college, and announced she was going to become a teacher of physical culture.

She was quickly forgotten, so we do not know what happened to her. Quite probably she did get married.

UP UNTIL 1904 a standard part of the scenery around home plate in major-league ball games was a long-handled broom. It was used, of course, by the umpires to sweep the dirt off the plate. And, like any other appurtenance of the game, a large body of superstition grew up around the kitchen-size broom.

When the umpire finished dusting off the plate he usually tossed the broom to one side. This casual act was always watched closely by the superstitious batsmen in the dugouts, for much depended on where that broom landed. If it was thrown to the right of the plate it foretold certain things about base hits or strike-outs, and if it landed to the left it meant something else again. The direction in which the handle might be pointing was sometimes sufficient reason for a manager to call for a change in strategy. On one occasion Hans Wagner wanted to change the position of the broom to help him get a hit; another Pittsburgh player protested on the grounds that if the broom were moved *he* would surely strike out. The two men got into a bitter quarrel over the matter.

Nobody thought of substituting the handier whisk broom for the tall variety until 1904. In that year a Chicago Cub named McCarthy was racing from third to home when he stepped on the broom and injured his ankle seriously. That was enough to outlaw the big broom. President H. C. Pulliam of the National League issued an executive order requiring that umpires use whisk brooms and stow them in their hip pockets. A year or so later the American League adopted the same rule.

WILLIAM A. HULBERT of Chicago was president of the National League for a number of years and one of baseball's greatest enthusiasts. When he died his friends and associates decided to erect a monument over his grave in Graceland Cemetery—a stone baseball, twenty inches in diameter and fashioned from red granite.

ONE AFTERNOON in 1889 the Yale baseball team journeyed down from New Haven to have a go at the Staten Island Athletic Club team.

At one point in the contest the Staten Island first baseman slipped a potato into his pocket before going to his position. Soon after that one of the Yales got a single. The first baseman held the runner close to the bag and finally the Staten Island pitcher threw the ball in an attempt to catch the collegian. The first baseman retained the ball and tossed the potato to the pitcher. The Yale man promptly took his lead off the bag and was as promptly tagged out.

There was an unseemly ruckus, of course, and the umpire ruled that the Staten Islander had been guilty of chicanery; moreover, the Athletic Club's governing committee called a meeting and reached the conclusion that the potato-hider was wanting in true sportmanship and a cad to boot, and his resignation was requested.

DAN BROUTHERS, a great star at first base for Detroit back in the 1880s, was putting on his coat at his home one morning, the time having come for him to leave for the ball park.

"Dan," said his wife, "I want you to get home early this afternoon."

"Can't do it," said Dan. "Double-header today. You ought to know that."

"Oh, dear," said Mrs. Brouthers. "Well, do what you can. We've cooked up a swell surprise party for you, and all your folks will be here."

"What's the big idea?" said Dan.

"It's your birthday, you big ape," said his wife.

Dan proceeded to the Detroit park and paid an immediate visit to Charles H. Byrne, president of the club. He asked Mr. Byrne if he might get away after the first game, inasmuch as this was his birthday and his folks were throwing a surprise brawl. Mr. Byrne said no. Mr. Byrne said that everybody has birthdays and that baseball is a business and that it is not the custom in American business life to dismiss employees early when they have a birthday.

Dan went grumbling. He played through the first game and during the intermission period sat with his teammates in the clubhouse. Mr. Byrne, walking through the room, noticed that Dan was morose and sullen, and Mr. Byrne decided to keep an eye on his first baseman for the remainder of the afternoon.

The club president's hunch had been right, for Dan had worked out a plan whereby he could get away early. In the second inning of the second game a looping foul fly came his way. Dan placed his hands in position for the catch, but permitted the ball as it came down to hit him on the head. Whereupon he fell to the sod and lay motionless.

A stretcher was brought onto the field and Dan was loaded up and carried slowly to the dressing room while the fans sat in sorrowing silence. Everyone in the park was sad about the matter except Charles H. Byrne. Mr. Byrne was not certain of his ground, but he suspected that Dan was anxious to get away and get to jiggin'.

So Mr. Byrne quietly left the ball park and stationed himself back of a tree which stood near the clubhouse entrance. In a little while Dan Brouthers, clad now in his street clothes, came hustling out of the clubhouse, headed for home. Out stepped President Byrne.

"You," he said, "can turn right around and get back into that clubhouse and get into your uniform and get on that bench and stay there till the last out is made."

While Dan was ruefully changing clothes again, President Byrne had an idea. He called the umpire to one side and said:

"I want you to do me a special favor. Brouthers faked that knock in the head so he could get away and go to a party. I know it's contrary to the rules, but I want to put him back to work. I want to make him work every minute for the rest of this game. We can't let these ballplayers get away with stuff like that."

The umpire was doubtful about such procedure at first, but agreed that Dan's conduct had been most reprehensible and that this was a special sort of case, so he arbitrarily suspended the rules and Dan went back into the game.

The rule-wise fans, of course, were perplexed, but before long the word got around, and everyone in the park knew what had happened. Dan had a great personal following, and the fans now went about the business of bringing a small ray of sunshine into his gloomy day. Volunteer collectors moved quietly through the stands, and soon a committee left the park. And in one of the late innings as Dan came to bat the proceedings were halted temporarily while another committee of admirers marched out bearing a tremendous birthday cake. The multitude arose and saluted him with an ovation, and in the midst of it stood Charles H. Byrne, applauding.

 FORTY and fifty years ago there was a strong belief, bordering on superstition, that a railroad train would never have a wreck so long as members of a baseball team were aboard it. This belief persisted and was held by railroad people as well as by a large proportion of the traveling public in an era when railway wrecks were far more numerous than they are today.

In 1911 an impromptu survey was made. The records showed that one ballplayer had been run over and killed by a train, another had died when his train was engulfed in the Johnstown flood, and a third had been run down by a train which cut off both his legs. None of these mishaps, said the report, could properly be described as a train wreck. And the report concluded:

"Traveling men, when they learn that they are to ride on a train bearing a ball club, do not take out accident-insurance policies for the trip. Railroad passenger agents like to have the patronage of ball clubs, not only for the additional revenue but because they figure the athletes' presence on the train is an omen that there will not be a disastrous wreck."

MANY baseball players have been superstitious about certain individual bats, but there has also been considerable hoodoo belief connected with bats generally.

Monte Cross, star shortstop for Philadelphia back in 1900, was one of many players who believed firmly in bat lore. Monte always studied the positions of the assorted bats which usually lay in front of the Philadelphia bench. If the handles of two bats were crossed, Philadelphia would surely lose the game in progress. Whenever it came time for Philadelphia to hit, Monte examined the row of bats on the ground. If the ends of two or three or more of the bats stuck out beyond the others, that indicated the number of runs Philadelphia would score during the inning.

Billy Bottenus, once a star performer for Cincinnati, is an example of the player who believed implicitly that every bat contained a certain number of base hits and no more. Because of this belief, Billy would never permit any other player to borrow his private weapons.

"I'm not going to let anybody else use up the hits in my bats," he said.

JOE JACKSON, at the height of his career, had eighteen bats and he treated them as if they were people. Each bat had a pet name, such as "Old Ginril" and "Big Jim" and "Caroliny." And each bat had certain attributes as well as certain shortcomings. Jackson once spoke of "Big Jim" in this wise: "He's comin' along good for a young feller, but I ain't got too much faith in him. Trouble is he ain't been up agin big-league pitchin' very long."

At the end of the 1913 season someone came upon Jackson busy packing his bats in several carrying cases. Joe said he was taking them to South Carolina with him for the winter. "Anybody," he added, "with any sense knows that bats are like ballplayers. They hate cold weather."

BEFORE modern baseball stands came into being, the "deadhead" problem was always a major worry to owners of ball clubs. In 1884 the owner of a Boston club thought he had licked the problem by erecting a high, stout fence around the park. But the fans who didn't believe in paying had one more trick to try. A line of telephone poles stood just outside the park, and whenever game time came dozens of men and boys were perched near the tops of the poles, where they watched the play without hindrance. At last the club owner had an idea. He waited until a game was under way, then sent out a crew of men with brushes and buckets of paint. Each pole was swiftly painted a bright wet red up to the point where the fans were clinging, and each of the deadheads ruined his clothes getting down. The poles were never used by spectators again.

A NEW WORD was introduced to baseball in 1886 and was taken up by the fans around Boston and Kansas City. The word was "ubbo."

Boston was playing at Kansas City, and an outfielder named Joe Hornung was coaching for the visitors. After Billy Nash got on first, Hornung suddenly mystified everyone by shouting, "Ubbo, Billy, ubbo!" Nash started to break for second base, but thought better of it.

Everybody figured that "ubbo" was some sort of a code word, and it was, but it happened that Weidman, the Kansas City pitcher, knew what it meant. As he wound up for the next pitch, Pitcher Weidman yelled over toward first base, "Ubbo!" Nash thought the cry came from Coach Hornung and set sail for second; the ball was waiting for him when he got there, and he was tagged out.

The mystery was cleared up at the conclusion of the game —a game in which the fans bellowed "ubbo!" almost constantly. Joe Hornung explained that "ubbo" was a term used by tramps, meaning "move along" or "get going." He had employed it as a signal to Billy Nash that he was to "get going" for second. He had not reckoned with the fact that Pitcher Weidman possessed a working knowledge of tramp argot, and Weidman used that knowledge to set a trap for the runner.

WILLIAM T. MADDEN of Louisville was a baseball fan, but his work as a locomotive engineer made it impossible for him to see many games.

He had a passenger-train run between Louisville and Cincinnati that took him past a baseball diamond at Gustig's Park

near Louisville, so there were occasions when he caught at least a glimpse of a ball game as he rolled by at a speed of forty-five miles an hour.

On a July afternoon in 1912 Madden's train approached the baseball field, and the engineer, as was his custom, leaned out of the cab window to have a good quick look at things. Just as his engine came abreast of the field, someone hit a high foul fly. Madden watched it, saw it come toward him, leaned out a little farther, and caught it with his bare hand. The crowd cheered, the locomotive fireman rang the bell, and Madden himself gave a few joyous toots on the whistle.

UNDER THE STRAIN of a tight game a ball-player may forget himself, may suddenly commit an act of impulse which is contrary to the rules. Such a case occurred in 1896 during a game between Cincinnati and Cleveland.

In the eighth inning Cincinnati was at bat. Irwin was on third, and Burke was on first for Cincinnati. Cy Young wound up and pitched, and Burke started for second. The Cleveland catcher made a beautiful throw to Childs, the second baseman. The throw was in time to catch Burke, but Childs somehow fumbled it, and it rolled away from him. Whereupon Irwin scored from third, and Burke decided to try to make it to third.

The second baseman at this point should have retrieved the ball and made an attempt to nip Burke at third. Apparently he was too excited to think straight. Here was Burke, rounding second and galloping for third. Childs didn't like that—didn't want Burke to get another base. So he forgot the ball and concentrated on the runner. He seized Burke, grabbing his legs with one hand and wrapping his other arm around the runner's torso. Then he tossed Burke high into the air. Perhaps he thought this action would serve to delay the runner, slow him down. It didn't slow Burke down. This flagrant violation of tactical rules, in fact, infuriated him. He rushed at the offending second baseman and began clouting him in the face—clouted him so expertly that he soon had Childs groggy.

Several thousand fans were rimmed around the outfield, and now they came charging in. Fortunately there were enough cops on hand to quell the riot—something more than a hundred policemen was standard strength at a ball game in those days.

NOWADAYS whenever a ballplayer is given a "day" by his fans, the gifts presented to him usually include such things as automobiles, television sets, electric hedge clippers, dolls that wet themselves, and cocktail shakers that can sing in a quartette.

Back in 1907 Miller Huggins, later to become manager of the New York Yankees, was playing second base for Cincinnati. One afternoon, facing the great Mathewson, little Huggins astounded everyone, including himself, by getting a home run. The fans celebrated the performance by presenting him with the following gifts: a pair of shoes, a gold watch, a five-pound box of chocolates, a scarf pin, and a Morris chair.

BASEBALL PLAYERS often pursue their occupation while they are asleep, judging from a long series of incidents that have been reported in the press from time to time. There have been several cases in which outfielders, dreaming of a hard run for a difficult fly ball, have leaped from their beds and gone sailing through the window. The most famous incident of this kind, however, involved John J. McGraw.

One winter day in 1910 McGraw went into a Herald Square barbershop for his daily shave. Relaxed in the chair, he soon went to sleep and got to dreaming about a close game. The barber was at work on McGraw's neck, and McGraw must have been back in Baltimore with the Orioles, for suddenly he leaped and flung up an arm. The action was so swift that his hand caught the razor, and then he rolled out of the chair and onto the floor. A chunk of his thumb was cut away, and there was a deep gash across the palm of his hand, but everyone in the shop considered he got off lucky—it was, they said, a miracle that the razor didn't slash his throat.

THE NUMBER-ONE FAN of the Pittsburgh Pirates during the season of 1904 was a man named Laird.

All through the first half of the season he rooted for his beloved Pirates, never missing a game when they were playing at home, shouting and urging them on toward the pennant. He continued in his optimistic mood when the Pirates began losing quite steadily. Then, as Pittsburgh's fortunes waned on the diamond, Mr. Laird's spirits fell in the grandstand. By August it became quite clear that the Pirates could not win the league championship.

Mr. Laird became increasingly despondent as his team continued downhill. Then on September 19 a Pittsburgh newspaper carried an item recalling the fervency of his devotion to the team and concluding with:

"Mr. Laird has been removed to the insane department of the Mercer County Almshouse."

CHARLIE GETZEIN was the pitching ace of the Detroit team which won the National League championship in 1887. He was also the major attraction when the team did a bit of barnstorming after the season ended.

At Sturgis, Michigan, where the champions were to meet the local team, Getzein was approached by a young man who said, "I'm on the Sturgis team, and a guy in this town has bet me ten dollars I won't make a run. If you'll pitch to me so I can score, I'll split my winnings with you."

"Fine," said Getzein. "Whadda you want me to do?"

"Throw one nice and easy down the middle," said the young man, "and I'll put it over the fence."

The Detroit pitching star was shocked at this suggestion.

"Oh no!" he said. "I couldn't do that. I couldn't leave a busher get a home run offa me." He thought for a moment. "Tell you what I'll do," he said. "I'll get two strikes on you and then throw the next ball over the catcher's head and out of the lot. All you have to do is swing on it for the third strike, then run down to first and on around the bases. That way you can score the run, and it won't look too much my fault."

This procedure seemed to suit the busher so well that he handed over five dollars to Getzein—before he himself had scored his run and collected his bet.

That afternoon the young Sturgis player stepped to the plate and faced the great Detroit pitcher. The boy seemed more confident than usual. Two strikes were called on him. Then Getzein wound up and cut loose a sweeping curve that crossed the plate chest high. The batter swung listlessly and heard the ball thud into the catcher's glove. "Strike three!" yelled the umpire.

When the game was cut short by rain, the bewildered young man sought out Getzein and demanded to know why he hadn't carried out his part of the scheme.

"You mean that was you up there?" exclaimed the pitcher. "Hell, I didn't reckanize you in your uniform."

And Charlie Getzein walked away five dollars wealthier.

BACK IN 1910 a baseball diamond was laid out in a field near the Lackawanna station at Harrison, New Jersey. One May afternoon a game was in progress on this field. A critical situation had arisen in the contest, and no one paid much attention to a train which was pulling out of the station bound for Hoboken. The bases were loaded and a slugger was at the plate.

The pitcher delivered, the batter swung, and the ball arched high and far toward left field just as the locomotive came huffing along. The left fielder sprinted toward the tracks, but the train's engineer saw him coming and gave a couple of warning toots on his whistle. The fielder stopped, saw the ball go over his head and drop into the smokestack of the locomotive. Four runs scored in spite of the vehement protests of the losing team. The umpire ruled: "All four runs count. That smokestack was in fair territory when the ball went into it."

MEMBERS of the old Baltimore Orioles had a reputation for fast thinking in the tight spots.

Brooklyn went down to Baltimore to play the Orioles one day in 1896. Came a point in the proceedings when Brooklyn had the bases filled. The next man up hit a grounder to Hughie Jennings at shortstop. Jennings threw wildly to the plate, and the ball somehow ended up in a water bucket near one of the dugouts.

Wilbert Robinson, the fabulous catcher, raced over to the bucket as Brooklyn's runners began charging around the bases. The bucket was full of water, and Robinson quickly decided against fumbling around in it for the ball. A small sponge was floating on top of the water, and Robinson grabbed it, whirled, and threw it to his pitcher, who had come down to cover the plate. The pitcher caught the sponge and slapped it with a squash on the person of Mike Griffin, who was charging into the plate.

The umpire, of course, called Griffin safe the moment he saw the sponge. But the important point was the fact that only one run scored—the other runners, thinking the sponge was the ball, held their bases.

FORTY YEARS AGO the management of the Pittsburgh ball park, disturbed about the expense involved through the loss of foul balls, hired an alert gentleman to stand in the street outside the stands and retrieve those balls that went out of the park so the kids could not get them. This gentleman on getting a ball was instructed to throw it back over the roof of the stands.

Boston was playing at Pittsburgh one afternoon and a Boston hitter named Bates fouled one over the roof. Just as Bates swung on the next pitch, the ball came sailing back from the street and landed squarely on top of Umpire Johnstone's head.

Meanwhile Tommy Leach caught the line-drive hit by Bates for the third out of the inning, and the Pittsburgh players trotted in toward their dugout. Umpire Johnstone, however, ordered them back to their positions. The ball that hit him on the head had stunned him momentarily, and he had not seen Leach catch the fly.

"Section four of rule twenty-eight," he announced, "says a play don't count if the umpire don't see it. I didn't see it. Go on back."

BASKETBALL TEAMS made up of members of a single family are not uncommon around the country today. In an earlier era, when families as a rule were larger, family baseball teams were operating in various parts of the country. Adrian Anson, who was to become a great star in the major leagues, got his start playing with a team made up of his relatives at Marshalltown, Iowa. The Nine Madden Brothers played a series of games in New England communities in 1878. And the Karpen Brothers, who ranged in age from sixteen to thirty-one, were a big attraction around Chicago in 1871. The Karpens came from Europe, and the boys learned to play baseball before they learned to speak English. Their mother was the team mascot. In 1890 the Karpens played the Lennon Brothers, an Illinois family team. And in 1903 these same Lennon Brothers, who lived at Joliet, Illinois, met the White Brothers of Hammond, Indiana, for the "family championship of the world." The Lennons won by a score of eighteen to one. At the end of the contest the parents of the winners, Mr. and Mrs. John Lennon, were given a great ovation. They had eleven sons and seven daughters.

Hughie Jennings, the Baltimore shortstop, came from a baseball family. The Jennings Nine, consisting of James Jennings and his eight sons, was playing ball around Wilkes-Barre, Pennsylvania, at a time when the father-manager (first baseman) was seventy-five years old.

IN THE TIME of baseball's antiquity, when the players liked their mustaches long and their beers tall, there occurred an incident in the nation's capital city which was argued over and fussed about for many years afterward. This was the case of the-ball-that-rolled-through-the-hole-but-couldn't.

Cap Anson brought his Chicago White Stockings into Washington for an important series of games, never suspecting that he'd leave town cussing a hole in a cellar door.

In one of the late innings of a memorable game Washington was at bat, trailing by one run, and had a man on third. The batter hit a sharp infield grounder. The shortstop fired the ball to the catcher in an attempt to cut off the run at the plate. The throw was a trifle wild, however, got away from the catcher, and rolled toward the base of the grandstand.

Directly in the path of that rolling ball was a sloping cellar door which marked the entrance to the passage by which the players reached their dressing rooms. Near the top of this door was a small hole through which a man could reach his fingers in order to pull a latch.

The vagrant ball rolled up the sloping door and disappeared into that hole. Meanwhile the man scored from third, and since there was no ground rule covering a hole in a door, the batter cruised merrily around the bases and crossed the plate with the winning run.

Cap Anson was in a fury. It wasn't legal, he cried. No goddam hole was gonna beat him out of an important ball game! He stormed around the field, severed diplomatic relations with the human race three or four times, and called the hole names that perhaps no other hole on earth was ever called.

The umpire stood his ground. He had with his own eyes

seen that ball drop through the hole. Everyone else, including several thousand spectators, had seen it. And when the wooden door was opened, there lay the ball at the foot of the steps leading into the passageway.

Suddenly Anson strode up to the hole. He seemed to be on the verge of kicking it, if a hole can be kicked. But he didn't kick it—he bent over and scrutinized it and then he called loudly for a baseball. A hush settled over the throng as he placed the ball over the hole and pushed. *A baseball would not go through that hole!* Anson grabbed a bat and tried to pound the ball through the hole. It still wouldn't go. Yet . . . yet . . . b'god a ball *had* gone through that hole!

Anson protested the game, but the decision of the umpire was approved officially. The pity of it all, it would seem, lies in the fact that the hole was not taken up and preserved as a museum piece, perhaps to end up at Cooperstown, properly mounted. Or can a hole be properly mounted?

THE NEW YORK *Herald* on July 21, 1915, carried the following dispatch out of St. Louis:

George Ruth today hit the longest home run ever seen at the American League park in St. Louis. Then he doubled twice and brought in three of the four runs with which Boston took the first of a seven-game series from St. Louis. The score was 4 to 2.

Ruth, on the slab for Boston, held St. Louis to two hits until the Browns filled the bases in the last inning with a walk and two singles.

Excellent fielding prevented St. Louis from scoring.

St. Louis threatened to tie the score when Ruth weakened. Wood relieved Ruth with the bases full and only one out and fanned two pinch hitters.

Ruth's home run in the third went clear over the right-field bleachers, across Grand Avenue, and landed on the far sidewalk.

AROUND the turn of the century at least two baseball clubs were at violent odds with Western Union. Charles Comiskey barred telegraphers from his park, arguing that transmission of play-by-play reports of the White Sox games was cutting down attendance.

Two years earlier the same situation arose in Baltimore, but the men of Western Union showed enterprise. Forbidden to enter the park, they erected a high platform just beyond the outfield fence and perched a telegrapher on it. The Baltimore management countered by raising a canvas screen which blocked the view from the platform. Not to be outdone, Western Union constructed another platform, this time on a wagon. For a few days there was more activity and more fun in the neighborhood of the outfield fences than there was on the playing field. The Western Union wagon would move into position. Out would go the canvas-hoisting crew. As soon as the screen was up the wagon would move to a new spot, and then the crowd would whoop as the canvas crew followed. The jockeying continued for several days, and then an agreement was negotiated under which the management agreed to admit telegraphers to the park provided they adhered to certain restrictions.

 A VISIONARY named Charles White came forward with a scheme in 1912 which would solve one of the major problems confronting the owners of baseball clubs. The owners were often complaining in those days about their inability to construct adequate playing fields owing to the high cost of real estate. Mr. White told them to quit worrying.

He submitted plans for a baseball field of immense proportions, sodded with bright green turf and containing all the other conveniences of an up-to-date ball field. This field, however, would be up in the air—built over the roof of the new Grand Central Station, extending from Lexington Avenue to Madison Avenue and from Forty-fourth to Fiftieth streets.

IN THE YEARS that he spent as an umpire in the National League Charlie Rigler had many an adventure; yet whenever it came time for yarning Charlie always preferred to tell the story of what happened to him at Annapolis.

It was the custom in those days for a major-league umpire to officiate at the annual baseball game between the Naval Academy and West Point. In this particular year Charlie Rigler got the assignment.

He was comparatively new at the umpiring business and he was not only proud of his Annapolis assignment but he was overflowing with a sense of importance.

As the time approached for the start of the game, Rigler left his dressing room; as he walked onto the playing field, a mighty roar went up—the spectators stood and cheered, and the bands played furiously, and there was much waving of banners and so on. Charlie was overwhelmed. This, he thought, is something! These people really appreciate the importance of an umpire. God love 'em!

"I turned around," he recalled, "and was just about to go into a modest bow, when I noticed something. The cheering crowd was not looking at me. They were looking at Teddy Roosevelt, who had just taken his seat in a box. Nobody had even noticed my arrival on the field."

TWO BASEBALL TEAMS composed of clergymen met one June afternoon in 1903 at Lacrosse, Wisconsin. Eastern newspaper accounts of the game describe the visiting team as coming from "Wiona" which may have been a misprint for Winona—a Minnesota city on the Wisconsin border not far from Lacrosse.

Of the contest the press dispatch said:

"In the last half of the fifth inning Rev. Van Ness of Wiona tried to steal second. Umpire T. M. Perham of West Salem, a professional player, ruled that he had been tagged out. Rev. Van Ness protested. Leonard Lotteridge, a venerable resident of West Salem, made a remark about babies, which was not clearly heard by the Wiona man.

"Don't you call me a sneak!" Rev. Van Ness shouted. "You Lacrosse men are not fair!"

The quarrel warmed, and the pastors gathered in an excited knot. Perhaps their remembrance of their official life was all that prevented a fight.

BASEBALL'S OBITUARY was written in 1881— on the editorial page of the New York *Times*, which in turn issued a clarion call for the country to adopt cricket as its national sport. The editorial follows:

There is really reason to believe that baseball is gradually dying out in this country. It has been openly announced by an athletic authority that what was once called the national game is being steadily superseded by cricket, and the records of our hospitals confirm the theory that fewer games of baseball have been played during the past year than were played during any other single year since 1868.

About twenty-five years ago there was an effort made to induce Americans to play cricket, but it failed. We were not at that time worthy of the game and in our ignorance we said, "Give us something easier." It was then that certain unknown persons resolved to take the old game of rounders, which had gradually become known by the name of baseball, and to make of it an easy substitute for cricket. To the latter game it bore much the same relation that the frivolous game of euchre bears to the grand science of whist.

The baseball conspirators said to their fellow countrymen, "Here is an easy game which everybody can learn. Let us play it and call it our national game." The suggestion met with a warm response, and baseball clubs sprang up all over the country.

Of course the national game soon lost the simplicity of the familiar baseball of country small boys. Elaborate rules were made and these were so constantly changed and so many additions were made to them that the study of baseball jurisprudence became a gigantic task.

When objection was early made to the national game that it was really fit only for boys, the conspirators hit upon the plan of using a ball about as hard as a ten-pound cannon ball and much more dangerous, and then proudly asked if they had not taken away the reproach that baseball was a small boys' game.

From that time on it became rather more dangerous to play baseball than to fill lighted kerosene lamps or to indulge in any other of our distinctively national sports.

It is estimated by an able statistician that the annual number of accidents caused by baseball in the last ten years has been 37,518, of which 3 per cent have been fatal; 25,611 fingers and 11,016 legs were broken during the decade in question, while 1,900 eyes were permanently put out and 1,648 ribs were fractured.

Had not the popularity of the game begun to decline some two years ago, it would undoubtedly have been demanded by Western Democrats that baseball cripples should be pensioned by the government, a measure which would at once bankrupt our national treasury.

During the halcyon period of the national game a number of enthusiastic players went to England in order to introduce it in that benighted land. They played several games in public, but the Englishmen refused to take any interest in the matter. They said, "Ah! Yes! Very nice game for little boys, but it's only our old game of rounders, you know." The American missionaries returned disappointed and somewhat disheartened, and from that time baseball began to show signs of waning popularity.

Then appeared the "professional players" to tell upon the game. They made a living by hiring themselves out to baseball clubs. They made what was originally designed to be a sport a matter of business. Worse than this, they made the national game a national instrument of gambling, and generally succeeded in placing it on a level with the game of three-card monte.

Games were won and lost in accordance with previous "arrangements." In other words, one set of players sold the game to their opponents before it was played, and the unfortunate people who had bets on the results were thus systematically robbed.

Of late years baseball has been rather more disreputable than was horse racing in the days before the existence of Jerome Park. The honest young men who dressed themselves in ridiculous uniforms, called themselves "Red-legs" or "White-legs," and broke their fingers by playing matches in public found that they were ranked in public estimation with professional black-legs. One need not wonder that they are now abandoning the game wholly to the professional players.

Probably the time is now ripe for the revival of cricket. The day has gone by when Americans looked upon athletic sports which really required muscle and endurance and upon games of cards in which intellectual effort was a more important element than chance as something to which they had no time to attend. Whist has to a large extent superseded euchre, and the latter has been banished from the drawing room to the railway smoking car.

Our experience with the national game of baseball has been sufficiently thorough to convince us that it was in the beginning a sport unworthy of men and that it is now, in its fully developed state, unworthy of gentlemen.

Cricket will probably become as popular here in the course of a few years as it is in England, and we shall be contented to play a game worth playing, even if it is English in origin, without trying to establish a national game of our own.

IN THE 1890s ballplayers often made a little money on the side by selling baseballs. Whenever possible a player would seize a ball and hide it in his blouse or perhaps in the grass. At the conclusion of the game it was an easy matter to dispose of the contraband. Small boys customarily gathered at the park exits, waiting with money in hand for the players to emerge, knowing that some of them would have balls to sell. In 1895 an executive of the Detroit team squawked bitterly about this practice, declaring, "It's unbelievable that ballplayers receiving two hundred dollars or more a month would crib balls to sell to the boys, but it is a fact that they do."

AROUND the turn of the century whenever a baseball pitcher began to have trouble with his pitching arm he usually headed for Youngstown, Ohio, and the shanty of Bonesetter Reese.

Reese was an obscure mechanic in Youngstown. In 1899 a big-league pitcher named Cuppy began suffering from severe arm pains which forbade his appearance on the mound. He consulted several specialists, but they didn't help him. Then a friend told him about the Youngstown mechanic "who studied anatomy for the love of it and set broken arms and legs after his regular working hours."

Cuppy went to Youngstown and sought out Bonesetter Reese. The mechanic fingered his arm a bit and then announced that "two of the cords are out of place." He took hold of the arm, gave it a couple of slight jerks and twists, and then told Cuppy he could pitch the next day. And Cuppy *did* pitch the next day without a suggestion of pain.

From then on many big-league stars beat a path to Bonesetter Reese's place. Newspaper reports of the time quote Youngstown physicians as saying that, while Reese was not a licensed doctor, they would not object to his "operations," because they were almost invariably successful.

A KENTUCKY "KERNEL" named Richard Whitehead seems to have been the outstanding baseball fan of the nation around 1905. Mr. Whitehead, a man of great wealth, lived for baseball.

Each spring he went to the training camp of the Louisville team and worked out with the players until the opening of the season. In those days the beginning of the season was customarily marked by a parade, and Mr. Whitehead, to be sure, was always in it, riding in his "fine auto carriage" and clothed in a Louisville uniform which he had tailored to his order.

Once the season was under way the Kentucky millionaire would return to his home town, Bowling Green, where he was sponsor of a semi-pro team. His club toured the state in elegance, putting up at the best hotels and usually traveling in the sponsor's private railroad car.

Questioned about his intense interest in the game, Mr. Whitehead made this declaration: "I would rather be the manager of a world's champion ball team than be the President of the United States and the King of England rolled into one."

SAGINAW was playing at Washington, Pennsylvania, one July day in 1896 with a bulldog present. The dog belonged to Manager Black of the Saginaw team, was the team's mascot, and, in fact, was named Saginaw.

The Pennsylvanians were leading, and Manager Black was unhappy and fretting. Came a moment when Saginaw got a man on first. The next batter hit a high foul, which was taken near the stands by the Washington catcher, Mitchell. The runner on first, seeing that Mitchell had his back to the field when he made the catch, took off in an attempt to make it to second, but the catcher was alert and threw him out.

Manager Black was fit to be tied. He was so furious over the way his rally had been halted that he jumped up and down and screamed. He looked around wildly for someone to blame, for someone to cuss. He couldn't blame the runner for trying to make second. He couldn't reasonably blame the batter for fouling out. He couldn't take out his anger on the umpire, for there was nothing wrong with the call at second. Yet he had to do something, and his eye fell on Catcher Mitchell—the man who had started the double play. There was the villain! Impulsively Manager Black grabbed up Saginaw, his bulldog, pointed him in the direction of Mitchell, and yelled, "Sick um, Sag! Go git 'im!" And Saginaw went for Catcher Mitchell. In his first leap the bulldog ripped Mitchell's stocking from knee to ankle, and Mitchell started running across the field. Saginaw chased him as far as second base and then concluded he had done his duty and turned around and went back to his master.

The umpire apparently hadn't heard Manager Black sick his dog on the catcher. Neither had the catcher, for when he returned to his post all he said was:

"It is my considered opinion that a baseball field is no place for a damn dog."

RAYDEN T. COLE, a deaf-mute printer of Dallas, Texas, attracted a lot of attention in 1907 with a proposal that organized baseball employ deaf mutes for umpires. His theory seemed to be that a man who could neither speak nor hear would make a perfect impersonal sort of arbiter, unaffected by curses and jeers, calling his decisions on the basis of sight and sight alone.

Mr. Cole, at the same time, revealed himself as an inventor. He was getting ready, he said, to patent a pneumatic base with a whistle attachment which would squeal the instant a player's foot touched the bag. And in addition to that Mr. Cole said he was working on a pneumatic hoot nanny to be worn by each player so that whenever a man was tagged, his clothes would let out a piercing shriek.

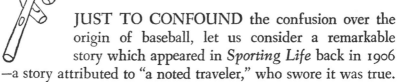JUST TO CONFOUND the confusion over the origin of baseball, let us consider a remarkable story which appeared in *Sporting Life* back in 1906 —a story attributed to "a noted traveler," who swore it was true.

On a June day in 1763 a small garrison of English soldiers occupied a stockade on Mackinac Island. The soldiers were loafing around inside the stockade when someone noticed a small group of Indians coming out of the nearby woods. It soon became apparent that the Indians were not bent upon attacking the fort; they had come into the clearing for the purpose of playing a game.

The game involved batting a ball with a stick and much running around, and the soldiers soon became interested in the proceedings and even began applauding. After a while the Indians motioned for the soldiers to come out and watch the contest at closer range. Some of them did, leaving the stockade gate open. The Indians said that the name of their game was "baggatiway."

The play continued for half an hour, and then an Indian took the stick and executed a fine piece of place-hitting. He clouted the ball and dropped it neatly within the walls of the stockade. All the Indian fielders now let out whoops and ran as if to retrieve it. The attack was so sudden and unexpected that all the soldiers but one were slain. The sole survivor, one Alexander Henry, escaped by hiding in a cave.

Anybody who doesn't believe this story is a tennis fan.

CRAZY SCHMIDT was a pitcher with a poor memory. Whenever he was at work on the mound he always had a little notebook in his hip pocket. As each batter came to the plate, Schmidt got out the book, riffled through it, and checked his private record of the man's potential weakness. One day in 1894 Cap Anson, four times batting champion of the National League, stepped to the plate and faced Crazy Schmidt. The pitcher got out his notebook and studied it a few moments. Then in a loud voice he read from it: "Base on balls." Anson walked.

LAVE CROSS, a veteran player who served with several big-league teams, was the man responsible for the rule, put into effect in 1895, restricting the weight and size of gloves that could be worn by fielders.

Cross had been catching for years when a situation arose in Philadelphia which saw him switched from behind the plate to third base. He took his catcher's mitt with him to his new position, arguing that he had been wearing it all his baseball life and saw no reason to make a change now.

Sizzling grounders were slammed at him, but they appeared to thump easily into his big glove, and he rarely missed a high fly. Opposing batters howled in anger when he continued stopping or catching balls that other third basemen couldn't have handled. In the end the rule makers went to work, and the restrictions as to glove weight and size were written into the book.

JUD SMITH, third baseman for Syracuse in 1897, was an unusual ballplayer. He did not cuss, smoke, chew tobacco, or drink. Yet he had one vice in common with his teammates—he was superstitious.

Jud got into a bad slump that season and went for weeks without getting a hit. He tried a wide variety of jinx-killers without success. Then one day the Providence club came to town, and Jud watched Bassett, the visiting team's third baseman, get a double and a triple on his first two trips to the plate. Jud decided to study Bassett's technique the next time he came to bat.

In the sixth inning Bassett once again walked to the plate, and Jud Smith's eyes were following his every movement. Just before Bassett stepped into the batter's box he reached in his hip pocket, pulled out a plug of tobacco, took a big chaw of it, put it back in his pocket, and hit the first pitch for a clean single.

"That's it!" said Jud to himself. "That's the secret!"

The next day Jud arrived at the ball park equipped with his own plug of tobacco.

Going up to hit in the first inning, he went through the Bassett routine, biting himself a chunk of tobacco, stepping into the box, and swinging on the first pitch. The ball went on a line to center field for a clean single.

Now let it be remembered that Jud Smith was not a skilled chewer of tobacco. As he made the turn for second base he stumbled slightly and swallowed the chew.

Within about fifteen minutes he was so sick that he had to be taken out of the game.

The story of what had happened got around, and a sports writer approached Jud that evening and asked him if he believed the tobacco trick would really break a batting slump.

"Sure," said Jud somewhat weakly. "No question about it. But far as I'm concerned, I'll stay in a slump till the end of the season rather than take another chew."

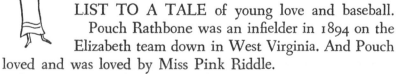

LIST TO A TALE of young love and baseball.
Pouch Rathbone was an infielder in 1894 on the Elizabeth team down in West Virginia. And Pouch loved and was loved by Miss Pink Riddle.

One great obstacle stood in their way. Miss Pink Riddle's papa and mama wanted no part of Mr. Pouch Rathbone. Their daughter, they said, deserved better from life than marriage to a ballplayer.

Pouch, however, was a man of action. Four times he tried to engineer an elopement; he even undertook the traditional course involving a ladder against a bedroom window—but, alas, the ladder broke and Papa Riddle shagged Pouch out of the neighborhood with a gun in his hand. There were other attempts at staging an elopement, but Papa Riddle now had a bulldog on the premises and after one unhappy encounter with the beast Pouch decided he'd have to try some other maneuver.

Now the peculiar thing about this situation was the fact that Papa and Mama Riddle were baseball fans. They liked the game, but they did not like the idea of having one of the performers in the family.

One day the Riddles dolled themselves up and got into their carriage and drove to the ball park to witness a contest between the Elizabeths and a team from Buring Springs. Papa Riddle did not know, of course, that a mighty plot was brewing and that the entire membership of the home team was involved in it.

The game was close and quite exciting—so exciting, in fact, that Papa Riddle did not notice during the seventh inning that Pouch had quietly left the Elizabeth bench and disappeared. Nor did he think anything of it when his daughter Pink, after waving and yoo-hooing at a girl friend named Martha in another part of the stands, excused herself and said she was going over to see this Martha.

Thus did Pouch and Pink disappear from view while the heated contest raged on; and now the Elizabeth team took up its part in the little drama. The players began deliberately to slow down the game because Pouch and Pink needed all the time they could get. A friend had been waiting for them outside the park, of course, with a buggy and a fast horse. Thus it was that they were able to cover a considerable distance before Papa Riddle reached the awful realization that he had been flimflammed. He was in an elegant fury. "Nobody," he roared, "would think the cad would elope in his baseball suit!" He rushed off to the telegraph office and wired the police of Parkersburg to apprehend the couple, for he felt almost certain that's where they would go. But Pouch and Pink anticipated his thoughts and crossed him up, driving to Marietta, Ohio. There they were wed—with Pouch Rathbone still in his baseball suit. A contemporary newspaper account of the affair concludes with:

> Mr. and Mrs. Rathbone arrived in Parkersburg from Marietta on the midnight train and put up at a hotel to wait until Mrs. Rathbone's parents invite them to return home. Pouch had gotten a new suit and presented quite a natty appearance. Receiving no word from the parents, they decided to proceed to Elizabeth. Arriving there yesterday, they were met by the entire population of the town. The courthouse was turned into a banquet hall, and hundreds paid congratulations and took part in the merrymaking.
>
> Mrs. Rathbone's parents relented.

AT ST. PAUL in 1908 William Beasley appeared in Ramsey County Court and asked for a divorce from Theresa Beasley. He charged her with desertion. His story:

"In the year 1900 I had to go away from my home on a brief business trip. When I returned my wife was gone. She left me a letter saying that she had joined a female baseball club and liked the sport so well that she would never return to me."

Divorce granted.

THE REV. CHARLES A. CRANE, pastor of the People's Temple in Boston in 1905, was doubtlessly a good man. He was a baseball fan and considered it part of his duty to elevate the game wherever possible, improve its tone, and cleanse it of whatever flaw he found in it.

One day the Reverend got to thinking about umpires. He knew that umpires were subject to almost constant abuse from the stands. He didn't like it. He thought something should be done to improve the lot of the umps. Thus ruminating, he evolved an idea and one day made public announcement of it.

Umpires, he said, were always catching old Ned from the fans because they were in a bad spot to do their umpiring. They shouldn't be on the playing field at all, said the Reverend.

"The umpire," declared the minister, "should be stationed up in the grandstand. There he would be able to see everything, and see it better than if he were down on the diamond."

Wouldn't that be glorious!

OLLIE CHILL, an American Association umpire, was officiating at a game in Louisville one afternoon in 1913 when a foul tip struck him on the foot. Ollie continued with his job, though the pain in the foot increased as the game went along.

Just before the ninth inning started Umpire Chill turned and spoke to the crowd. He said that if there was a doctor in the stands he would appreciate it if said doctor would come to the umpire's dressing room after the game and examine his foot.

When the umpire reached the dressing room he found nineteen men awaiting him. He sat down and took off his shoe and sock and held his injured foot out toward the group crowded in the little room. One by one, each of the nineteen stepped up and examined the foot, then stepped back without saying anything.

Finally Ollie Chill became suspicious. He began asking questions. Among those nineteen men there was not a single doctor. Each man admitted that he had responded because "I always wanted to see what an umpire looked like up close."

IN 1911 the Detroit Tigers were told that they should try to forget about Harold Lockwood, King Baggott, Mary Pickford, John Bunny, Alice Joyce, and Harry Carey. Manager Hughie Jennings advised his players that "picture shows" were bad for the eyesight and that they should stay away from them.

KNOTTY LEE, a pitcher in the International League, was setting ball parks afire with both his hurling and his hitting during the first part of the 1906 season. Then tragedy befell him in a game at Worcester.

"I never was much good," Knotty sometimes remarked, "after the day I got kilt."

Mr. Lee was "kilt" in action. He was going great guns on the mound that day, when one of the batters drove the ball straight back at him navel high. It hit him in the pit of the stomach. He started falling forward, and instinctively his hand seized the ball; when his teammates got to him he was lying on the ground unconscious. The fact that the ball was held in an iron grip in his hand and had to be pried loose was sufficient evidence for several of the players to believe that Knotty was dead—they believed that only dead men need to have their hands pried open. The report ran through the crowd, therefore, that Knotty Lee had been "kilt."

They picked up his unconscious form and carried him away to a hospital. Twenty-six hours passed before Mr. Lee opened his eyes and asked the customary question, "Where am I?" In a very short time he was strong and chipper, and his wife was allowed in to see him and to show him all the telegrams of condolence she had received, plus the beautiful obituary tributes that the newspapers had carried.

THE TERM "Charley horse" belongs to baseball. It is possible to get a Charley horse in a game of ping-pong or milking a cow or during a love affair; but the expression is commonly used in baseball.

H. L. Mencken in *The American Language* reports on his efforts to trace the term's origin, which has long been in dispute. So far as he could determine, Mr. Mencken wrote, "Charley horse" had been traced back to 1891. He offered two versions of its origin.

Bill Clarke, who was a first baseman for the old Baltimore Orioles, said the expression came from the name of Charley Esper, a left-handed pitcher who walked like a lame horse. An ex-catcher in the Western League argued that it was first used in Sioux City, Iowa, and was suggested by a horse used at the local ball park by a grounds keeper named Charley.

At the awful risk of being called scholarly, this book's research expert dived head first into the archives of the Library of Congress and emerged with what appears to be the final word in the matter.

The man who coined the expression "Charley horse" was Joe Quest, an infielder with Chicago in the early 1880s.

The man who had the first Charley horse that was called a Charley horse was an outfielder named Gore, playing with the same team.

One day in the summer of 1882 the Chicago team had an open day, and several of the players got up a party to attend the races. On the way to the track a couple of the boys started talking about a hot tip they had on a horse named Charley. Everyone in the group was interested except the aforementioned infielder, Joe Quest. When the ballplayers got up a pot to bet on the horse Charley, Joe Quest was the only man who refused to contribute. Consequently he was subjected to a lot of ribbing by the others and he, in turn, snorted at them and called them suckers.

Hugh Nichol, an outfielder, later told the story of the race. He said that Charley took the lead right at the start and that Mike Kelly, who was along and who had a bet on the nag, began whacking Joe Quest with his cane and yelling, "Look at him go! Too bad you're so dumb, Joe!" Charley was still far in front when he reached the stretch and then, of course, he began to stumble a bit and finally pulled up, lame in his right hind leg. He finished last.

Now, to be sure, it was time for Joe Quest to crow.

"What do you think of your old Charley horse now!" he bellowed, and all the way back to town he kept up the cry, "Oh, Charley horse! What a fizzle!"

The following day the team met New York on the old Chicago lake-front grounds. Chicago was leading by one run in the fifth inning, and Joe Quest was coaching at third base.

Gore led off the inning and got a single. On the first pitch to the next batter Gore broke for second. Halfway down the line his foot hit a soft spot on the base path, and he came up lame. He was thrown out at second and as he limped off the field, Joe Quest began taunting him in a playful manner.

"Just a Charley horse!" yelled Joe. "Just an old Charley horse!"

Gore was out of the lineup with his bad leg for several days and when anyone asked him about his injury he rarely got a chance to discuss it, because his teammates would sing out, "Just a Charley horse!"

Thereafter, whenever a member of the team hurt the muscles of his leg the injury was called a Charley horse, and the expression caught on elsewhere in baseball.

Joe Quest quit baseball and in 1887 had become a sports writer in Cleveland. In that year a Chicago sports writer began publishing a series of kidding articles aimed at Joe and blaming him for inventing an ailment among ballplayers which, said the Chicago writer, was all too often imaginary.

NEVER turn around real suddenly when you hear your name called or for any other reason. Might break both your kneecaps.

This warning is inspired by the experience of a man named King, who was once an umpire in the American League. King had been an outfielder, but he had to abandon playing and take up umpiring after his misfortune. He said that he had once been running to catch a fly ball. Reaching a point where he believed the ball would drop, he put on the brakes, then whirled around. Without hitting anything, without falling, he broke both kneecaps.

Hey, Pegler!

154

FRANK CHANCE, in the days when he was managing the Chicago Cubs, didn't agree with many of his fellow managers that betting on horses was demoralizing to baseball players. His opinion, as stated in the press, was: "I figure that a little bet now and then results in moderate excitement which, I really believe, helps to stir up mental activity."

JACK CHESBRO, star pitcher for the New York Americans in 1905, had a side job of coaching pitchers on the Harvard University team.

One night Chesbro had a dream. It was a dream about a ball game in which the pitcher was putting on an unusual performance—he was standing on second base and pitching to the plate and burning them across, at that. Even in the dream Jack Chesbro figured this to be a real cutie-pie performance, so he took a close look at the long-distance pitcher and said to himself, "Hell, that's Coburn!"

The next day Chesbro gave some thought to his dream. The pitcher he had envisioned was Coburn, and Coburn was a boy who had been giving him some trouble lately. Coburn had all the makings of a great pitcher, save for one important flaw—he couldn't seem to get his ball to break until after it crossed the plate. So the dream gave Coach Chesbro an idea.

He stationed Coburn about fifteen feet back of the mound toward second base and had him curve balls from that point. After a while he moved him in a couple of feet and had him throw some more. Gradually he worked the boy in to his proper position on the mound and, somehow, the procedure solved the problem; Coburn's curve broke as it should, and he went on to become one of the best pitchers Harvard ever had.

At least that's the way dreamer Chesbro always told it.

SINCE WORLD WAR II there have been ball games staged between one-armed and one-legged veterans. Such a thing is not new. Back in September of 1887 the same kind of game was played at Philadelphia. The players were railroad men who had been crippled in accidents. Those with one arm were called Snorkies, while the one-legged team was known as the Hoppers. The Snorkies won the contest, 35 to 14.

Noteworthy among the special problems which arose during the game was the hot dispute on a play at first base. A Snorkie hit a ground ball to short and lit out for first. The Hopper shortstop made a nice fielding play and threw to his first baseman. The throw was a trifle wide, but the Hopper first baseman caught it and touched the bag with his crutch. The base runner set up a howl—contending that the crutch was not a part of the first baseman. The umpire ruled that it was and declared the runner out.

A SPORTSCASTER of our own time occasionally mentions the skill of a certain pitcher who has what the radioman calls "a marvelous nothing ball." In explaining the thing the sportscaster has never made it crystal clear, to one listener at least, just what the "nothing ball" is. It is either a ball that appears to have lots of stuff on it but, in reality, has nothing on it and therefore baffles the batter; or it is a ball that appears to have nothing on it, but, in reality, has lots of stuff on it and therefore baffles the batter. Regardless of the explanation, everyone must agree that a "nothing ball" is a great achievement.

Special pitches have had special names down through the years, and one is worth noting in particular. Back around 1915 the St. Louis Browns drafted a pitcher named Perryman from the Atlanta club. Perryman was described as a young man who entered professional baseball for the sole purpose of accumulating enough money to put himself through a theological seminary so that he might become a clergyman. He had a fast ball with a peculiar hop. It was called by those who had trouble hitting it "Perryman's halo ball."

 IN THE PRE-DAWN era before psychoanalysis, baseball fans often recognized the presence of certain mysterious qualities which governed the behavior of their heroes on the diamond.

Johnny Evers, the great second baseman for the Chicago Cubs, was one of the players whose special qualities were often discussed by fans and sports writers alike. They talked of his antic liveliness, his "pepper," and his "dynamic energy." There came a time, finally, when a great many people believed that electricity was responsible for Johnny's incomparable verve.

In the beginning the fans would remark knowingly, "See ole Johnny Evers out yonder? They say he's all charged up with a lotta 'lectricity buzzin' around in him. Wouldn't doubt it at all, at all." And from that the legend grew until one would have thought that Johnny Evers was an article turned out by Mr. Edison in his Jersey laboratory.

Whether Evers himself believed he was supercharged with electricity is not known. He was aware of the stories, of course, and he certainly helped them along and contributed to them.

He announced one day that he did not want any of his admirers to give him any more watches; he was always being presented with nice watches, but they were no good to him. The minute he started carrying a watch, he said, it ceased to give accurate time—the electrical currents in his body fouled up the mechanism.

At least one sports writer took him seriously, for he wrote:

"That just seems to indicate that there is something unusual —some special kind of energy currents—that you find in ballplayers who are exceptionally endowed with vim and liveliness."

THE MODERN-DAY strip-tease girls who specialize in "bumps" and "grinds" could have learned a few movements if they had been privileged to watch John Clarkson pitch a ball game. Clarkson was one of the game's great pitchers in his day, and his physical maneuverings were nothing out of the ordinary until one day he got a big idea. He bought himself a whopping buckle for his belt, made of silver, and he always kept it polished to a dazzling glitter. It was his notion that the reflection from the buckle would dazzle the batters who faced him.

He soon realized that the buckle had to be in a precise position in order to reflect light into the batter's eyes, and he could never be certain himself just when it *was* in the right spot. So he took to wiggling his body just before he pitched, executing

his own bumps and grinds and hula jerks, trying to make certain that the reflection would blind the batters. Those who watched him pitch during his buckle period say nothing like it was ever seen before on a diamond or elsewhere. Eventually, when batters started complaining, Clarkson was deprived of his big buckle, but it took him a long time to get over the habit of wiggling furiously before each windup.

THE STRAIN under which baseball players sometimes work, especially when they are driving toward a goal which demands that there be no faltering, is exemplified in the story of Rube Marquard's 1912 performance.

Rube won nineteen games in a row for the New York Giants that year—a record that still stands. When the Cubs finally beat him and ended his winning streak, Rube's teammates actually felt like celebrating.

"If," said one of them, "it had gone on any longer, Rube would have ended up in the nut house—and some of us with him."

There came a time during the streak when, each time he pitched, Rube's mind was constantly dwelling on the possibility of defeat—and the same thoughts were in the minds of his teammates. Every time a batter hit a fly ball Marquard stood on the mound with his eyes closed, his teeth clenched, and his fists knotted at his sides. Very often he didn't even realize when a third out had been made, and once Herzog had to lead him off the mound to the bench. He got so he stumbled around as if in a daze. Once he picked up a sweater and wrapped it around his right arm instead of his pitching arm, as was his custom. Sometimes he seemed to have trouble putting his cap on his head.

"I couldn't think of anything else while I was awake," Rube himself said when it was over. "And at night I couldn't sleep, and if I did sleep, I got nightmares—the air was full of balls, gloves, and bats, and players were running at me like they were going to kill me. And all night long I pitched ball. It was awful."

THE PUBLISHER of the Chicago *Tribune* got so hopping mad one day in 1881 that he announced, "I am never again going to permit an item of baseball news to appear in my newspaper."

He was outraged over the news that a Chicago team had played a game at Troy, New York, at the very hour when the funeral services and burial of President Garfield were taking place.

ONE OF the greatest names in American baseball is Jack Keefe, the letter-writing pitcher in Ring Lardner's classic, *You Know Me, Al.* Jack was a man of many elaborate tragedies, and you may recall that one of his great moments of despair was brought on by his infant son Little Al. The baby was no more than a couple of weeks old when he started waving his arm around in the air. *And it was his left arm.* The prospect of having a left-hander in his family all but killed Jack Keefe. He had rather, he said, have a X-eyed baby than a left-hander.

Heywood Broun, himself a left-hander, once wrote an essay in defense of southpaws. The very fact that he wrote it suggests that they needed a defense.

Back in 1892 the newspapers discussed left-handedness among ballplayers at considerable length, inspired by the "findings" of a certain Dr. Burton, who was described as an expert on the anatomical peculiarities of athletes.

"Man," said Dr. Burton, "is naturally right-handed, and for that reason the right side of the body is always more fully developed and better able to stand a constant strain than the left side. What is more, a left-handed man may be regarded somewhat in the light of a freak, an unusual thing in nature. Also the swing of the left side is more likely to affect the heart than similar motions with the right side."

His conclusion: left-handed pitchers have shorter careers than right-handed pitchers.

CHRIS VON DER AHE, the St. Louis saloonkeeper who became boss of the St. Louis Browns, was a man with a terrible temper.

One day Kid Gleason fumbled a ball in the field, and Chris got into such a rage over it that he told his bookkeeper to impose a fine of $100 on Gleason. The money was to be withheld from the player's next salary check.

Came payday, and Gleason arrived in Von der Ahe's office, screeching. What the hell did the boss mean by withholding a hundred dollars from his pay? Chris told him.

Gleason grew even more furious and went into a sort of crouch, as though ready to spring upon Chris. His features grew mildly purple as he shrieked:

"I'm countin' three! If you don't hand me that hundred dollars by the time I get to three I'm gonna knock your doddern teeth down your doddam throat! One . . ."

"Don't count!" cried Chris. "Here iss der money! It was chust a little choke! You are happy now?"

IN THE BEGINNING a baseball writer was not a man much given to poetic forms of expression. He usually confined his reports to straightaway factual accounts of the games. As early as 1867, however, the baseball writer was beginning to acquire importance in the journalistic field.

That year the National Club of Washington made baseball history by setting out on a barnstorming tour of the country. And a New York newspaper, the *Sunday Mercury*, made journalistic history by sending a staff man on the trip so that it might print daily telegraphic reports of the tour.

The first dispatch came from Columbus, Ohio, where the Nationals played the Columbus Capitals. The score was 90 to 10 in favor of Washington. An even hundred runs were scored, despite the fact that the game was called at the end of the seventh so the local team could entertain the visitors at a banquet.

A noteworthy feature of this first dispatch from the road was the fact that no name of any player was mentioned in it. Let us come down now to 1884 and examine a story composed by a sports writer in Boston—a story about a player named James White. There is a strong suggestion that personal prejudice had finally shown its ugly face in the realm of sports writing. A careful study of the following brief essay leads one to suspect that the author of it was biased in favor of the man he was writing about. Of course we could be wrong. Judge for yourself:

> Placid like the frog pond on a moonlit evening, quiet as the growth of grass upon a hero's tomb, unassuming as the innocent cow that munches the wholesome cud, is the

theologian of the baseball profession, honest James White.

Years have passed, pennants have been won and lost, even the grandstand has changed, and the Boston & Providence Railroad has found some new cars; but James is all by himself, the same genial, simple-hearted person he was in days of yore.

Faithful James! He remains where others have perished. Gone is the Chicago quartette that robbed Boston of its glory in 1876. Barnes is swallowed up in the metropolitan grandeur of Rockford, Illinois. Spalding has grown fat and forgotten the traditions of his former days. McVey, the much-loved, has disappeared, whither none knows. But White remains and moistens his palm for a drive to the field.

THE NEW YORK MEMBER of this firm remembers a Sunday morning some years back when he was aboard a subway train on the lower west side of Manhattan. At a station near one of the Jersey ferries the car doors opened and in came an entire baseball team, wearing uniforms and carrying equipment. It appeared to be some kind of semi-pro outfit bound for a ball park uptown. Every one of those ballplayers headed for a seat, dropped into it, and promptly went to sleep. The reporter who witnessed this performance didn't know at that time that ballplayers, as a rule, are among the sleepin'est people on earth.

Back in the 1890s, in fact, a sports writer composed an essay on the subject, raising the question: "Why is a ballplayer's life so soporific?"

"The New York players," he wrote, "are exceptionally temperate in the use of stimulants, but every one of them sleeps on an average of ten hours out of each twenty-four, and a few put in twelve hours with regularity. Even at that luxurious rate, half of the members of the team put in the rest of the day, when they are on trains, indulging in dozes."

 YESTERDAY'S BALLPLAYERS often had business or professional interests away from the diamond, just as they do today. From the old newspaper files come occasional items dealing with these extracurricular activities.

Chick Stahl of Boston, for example, obtained a patent on a combination washtub stand and ironing board; during road trips he spent his spare hours hustling around each city engaging agents to sell his product.

The famous Johnny Evers was getting personal publicity around 1907 for having perfected a method making it possible "to iron a celluloid collar without setting it on fire."

A Boston paper reported on off-the-diamond talents of contemporary stars in 1906. Frank Chance was the best boxer; Hal Chase excelled at billiards; Noodles Hahn was a fine piano player; Hans Wagner knew not his peer at pinochle; Jake Beckley was known as a gourmet; John McGraw was a scholar, specializing in racing forms.

Larry Lajoie in the time when he was managing Cleveland published baseball literature on the side. Harry Bemis of the same team carried an extra valise filled with books on the art of embalming, having decided to become an undertaker. George Stowall was a skilled butcher, and Harry Bay was a cornet player of some talent.

"Leaping Dave" Altizer of the Chicago White Sox infield came up in 1908 with a gismo which brought him some extra spending money. It was a post card bearing a picture of William Jennings Bryan. When held up to the light, the White House appeared alongside Bryan.

The New York press once got up a list of men who had pitched no-hitters in the past, and then looked around to see what had become of them. Some, of course, were dead, some were still pitching in the major leagues, and a few were in the minors. Among the others, Ward was a lawyer, Donahue a hotelkeeper in Philadelphia, Hahn a surgeon in Ohio, Rusie a ditchdigger in Indiana, and John Clarkson was confined to an insane asylum. Kilroy was running a saloon in Philadelphia, Callahan owned a ball club in Chicago, Morris owned a poolroom in Pittsburgh, and King was laying brick in St. Louis.

Jake Wells, who had played first base for Detroit, became a theater magnate in the South and eventually was rated as a millionaire. John K. Tener, once a big-league pitcher, became a member of Congress, and E. M. Lewis, who pitched for Boston, wound up as a professor at Williams College.

David Livingston Fultz, one-time star outfielder for the New York Americans, was a versatile man away from the diamond. He lectured, played the piano, sang bass, was an expert swimmer, and had been a football star at Brown University. He retired from baseball to become a lawyer.

Hubert "Dutch" Leonard was good on the trap drums, while Sam Crawford, the hard-hitting outfielder with Detroit, was a barber by trade.

In 1906 Umpire Tim Hurst turned inventor. One day he took a ride on a sight-seeing bus in New York City, and the experience set him to thinking. Why, he pondered, should people have to ride all over hell and back to find out what New York City looks like? Then he had his big inspiration. He devised a stationary sight-seeing tour of the city. It involved huge rolls of canvas which were slowly unwound before the eyes of the customers. On the canvas were painted scenes of the city such as might be viewed from a bus. Somehow Umpire Hurst's project failed to make him a fortune.

Concluding, there was Amos Rusie. In 1894 Amos was being paid the "fabulous" salary of four thousand dollars a year as a pitching ace for New York. A few years later he was found working for a dollar and a half a day in a lumberyard at Vincennes, Indiana. "This is the kind of life for me," he told a reporter. "I'm living in peace and quiet with my family and I'm happier than I ever was in baseball." It developed later, however, that Amos was not averse to improving his lot. He moved from Vincennes to Cairo, Illinois, where he got a job that paid him four dollars a day.

IT IS NECESSARY to cross the continent and invade California in order to find a record of a baseball game in which not a single player gave the umpire any argument. The game was played around 1906 in Alturas, with Cedarville as the visiting team. The rivalry of the two clubs was traditional—their meetings in the past had been characterized by fist fighting and, on occasion, assaults upon umpires. The feeling was running high this time too.

Just before the start of the game the umpire called all the players to a conference around home plate and there delivered a little lecture.

"You fellows," he said, "are going to play baseball and that's all. No monkey business. No fighting. And *no hollering at me!*

Get that straight. The first bird who steps out of line will have me to deal with, and I mean business."

That umpire was the sheriff of the county, with his hip pockets full of blackjacks and a gun stuck in his belt. It was the most peaceable baseball game the people of Alturas ever witnessed.

THE LADIES of Cincinnati were just wild about Tony Mullane. Tony was a pitcher for the Reds in the 1890s, and it was agreed all around that he was the handsomest ballplayer on earth. One day the management suddenly realized that Mr. Mullane's presence on the mound was a guarantee that hundreds of females would flock to the park who otherwise would stay home with their tatting. Thus it came about that all during the season the women's pages of the local newspapers frequently carried small ads which said simply, "MULLANE WILL PITCH FOR CINCINNATI TODAY."

THE BROOKLYN fans simply couldn't understand it—why Umpire Hank O'Day let Bill Dahlen get away with it.

Dahlen was one of their heroes, being a top star on the Brooklyn team; still and all, it wasn't like Hank O'Day to let a player cuss him and make like he was gonna spit all over him.

All through the first game of a double-header that day long ago Dahlen kept up the running fire of abuse against the umpire. Once he stamped on O'Day's foot. Once he threw a handful of dirt at the umpire. And Umpire O'Day just made as if nothing was happening.

Later on the story came out. Before the start of the first game Bill Dahlen approached Hank O'Day in a friendly spirit.

"Hank," he said, "suppose a player started callin' you a so-and-so and a such-and-such in the first game today. What would you do?"

"I'd throw the so-and-so and the such-and-such outa the game and outa the park," said O'Day.

"That's fine," said Dahlen. "I got an itch to get away this afternoon about the middle of the first game. Want to go out to the track and see the horses run. Want me to put down a little bet for you?"

"No, thanks," said Umpire O'Day.

So Dahlen started abusing the umpire in the early innings of the first game, but O'Day had decided that, come what may, he wasn't going to play into Dahlen's hands—Dahlen was going to no horse races that afternoon if he could help it. So he ignored the abuse, and by the time the second game had started Dahlen realized he'd never make it to the track and resigned himself to baseball.

FRED CLARKE, playing manager of the Pittsburgh Pirates, stole home one day in 1906, but didn't know he was doing it.

Pittsburgh was playing Chicago and had the bases loaded, with Clarke occupying third. The count on the batter stood at three balls and one strike. Standing on the base path, Clarke watched the next pitch cross the plate. The umpire made no sound or gesture, and the pitch looked high and wide to Clarke, so he assumed it was ball four, forcing over a run. Manager Clarke, therefore, simply strolled down the line and across the plate.

The batter, observing that his manager was walking in from third, also assumed the pitch was ball four and he ambled down toward first. And the Chicago catcher, witnessing these operations, reached the same conclusion.

Just as Clarke crossed the plate and as the scorekeeper was recording the run in his book, the umpire threw back his shoulders and bellowed:

"Strike two!"

Then he turned around and, slightly shamefaced, said:

"Had a dern frog in my throat. Couldn't speak a word."

Now that he could speak a word, he ruled the run was legal, and Clarke was given credit for stealing home with the speed of a mud turtle.

 DURING the early years of this century there was a catch phrase among the Pittsburgh players: "Don't let Barney give you any ether."

The reference was to Barney Dreyfuss, long president of the Pittsburgh club, and to an incident involving one of the players, Jess Tannehill.

Tannehill injured his shoulder badly while engaged in an impromptu wrestling match one day with a teammate. President Dreyfuss summoned a doctor and stood by while the physician diagnosed the trouble. A minor operation was needed, and Tannehill was given ether.

While he was under the anesthetic, Tannehill did some talking. He revealed that there was a lot of internal dissension in the club and considerable plotting against Dreyfuss. At least one player, a capable catcher, was fired, and a number of others were penalized as a consequence of Tannehill's anesthetic.

RUBE MARQUARD had set a new world's record of nineteen consecutive victories as a pitcher during the season of 1912, when he and the New York Giants faced the Cubs at Chicago on July 8. From the way things looked in the first inning everyone agreed that Rube would add another win to his string before the afternoon was over.

In the second inning, while Rube was on the mound, strange noises began coming from a tree that grew just beyond the fence. A woman had climbed into the tree and now she was perched in its branches, waving a shawl and performing like a witch on a broom, screaming insults at Rube Marquard. Her shrieking voice penetrated every corner of the field, and all her abuse was directed at the great Giants pitcher. By the sixth inning Marquard was so upset and nervous that he lost his control and had to be replaced.

The woman kept up her shrieking until the game was over, when a large crowd gathered at the foot of the tree. She continued screaming insults until the fire department arrived, dragged her out of the tree, and carted her off to a hospital for the insane.

A Chicago newspaper, reporting the incident, said that when Marquard reached the dressing room—his winning streak ruined by the tree shrew—he said, "That poor woman certainly put the jinx on me. Her shrill voice affected me so deeply that I just simply could not do a good job of pitching."

What Marquard *really* said is not known at this late date.

THE DETROIT management issued an announcement in 1896 saying that in the future its ticket booths would be occupied by ladies. The announced reason: "The average woman is more honest than the average man; the men may nearly always be counted upon to hold out overchange."

(The co-authors of this book are happy to report that the Detroit team didn't come within ninety miles of the pennant that year. The scum!)

UP IN the state of New Hampshire the communities of Keene and Hinsdale hated each other, many years ago, for baseball reasons.

Whenever the two teams met there were always arguments and fights and sometimes rioting on the part of the fans.

One day in 1898 Hinsdale journeyed to Keene for a renewal of the feud. In the fourth inning Alfred G. Doe (there *are* people in this world named Doe) came to bat for Hinsdale and faced Bill Griffin, who was pitching for Keene.

Griffin threw the ball, and it hit Doe in the ribs, whereupon Doe threw his bat at the pitcher. The two players rushed at each other and started slugging. A howl went up from the stands, and Alfred G. Doe heard it and knew what it meant. He was in enemy territory and he used the better part of valor. He abandoned his disagreement with Pitcher Griffin and started running. He raced out of the park, and behind him came a screaming mob of Keene fans.

Doe was fast on his feet and put some distance between himself and the mob. Finally he turned a corner and saw a house

with the front door standing open. He rushed inside and the lady of the house, Mrs. Tom Finan, listened to his story and agreed to harbor him until such time as matters cooled off and he could get out of town.

Thereafter for many years a large package arrived at the home of Mrs. Finan a few days before each Thanksgiving. It always contained a plump turkey and it always was postmarked Hinsdale, New Hampshire.

IT IS a common thing to hear ballplayers complain about the horrors of travel. And it is probable that Red Killifer, who used to play in the American League, did some bellyaching on the subject back in 1909.

Manager Hughie Jennings of the Detroit Tigers came to Killifer one day and told him he was to report to Montreal.

Red arrived in Montreal to find that the team was playing in Rochester.

He made his way to Rochester, where he was told that the holdout player whose position he was supposed to fill had come to terms. The Rochester manager suggested that Red go back to Detroit.

He started back for Detroit after wiring ahead and en route got a telegram from Hughie Jennings ordering him to report to the Baltimore club.

Arriving in Baltimore, Red found that the team was playing in Providence.

He took a train for Rhode Island and got to Providence just as the Orioles were ready to climb aboard a train and travel back to Baltimore.

Arriving again in Baltimore, Red found a telegram awaiting

174

him—another wire from Jennings—this time telling him he was needed in Detroit.

Reaching Detroit, he had only one thing to say. "Baseball's a great game, but damn if I like the travel part of it."

THE MANAGEMENT of the New York Giants was happy when the last out was finally made in a game with Pittsburgh one afternoon at the Polo Grounds in 1907.

Among the incidents over and above the scoring of runs were these:

Catcher Bowerman of the Giants was hit in the head by a pitched ball and had to be taken to a hospital.

A man in the bleachers threw a fit.

Bresnahan of the Giants was injured.

Doyle of the Giants was hurt.

Dahlen of the Giants was hurt.

Phelps of the Pirates was hurt.

Fire broke out in the upper stand.

A bucket brigade was formed, and the water used to put out the fire upstairs doused the spectators in the lower sections.

When it was all over there were sighs of relief from the Giants high command, remarks such as, "Thank God this day is over!"

But the day was not over. That evening the fire started up again, and about sixty feet of the grandstand had to be ripped down in order to get at the blaze.

Who won? Can't say. The newspaper account neglected to mention the score.

WHAT BASEBALL FAN of today remembers the name of Scoops Baedler?

Very likely it stirs no memories anywhere. He was only a third baseman for Canonsburg in the Allegheny and Washington League back in 1911. Scoops, however, deserves something better than the obscurity his name now enjoys.

The Canonsburg manager was not overly fond of him—accused him of "loafing" on the field and even hinted that he might have been involved in a plot to throw a game or two.

The league president, W. B. McVicker, conducted an investigation and was inclined to give Scoops Baedler the benefit of the doubt. McVicker suggested that if Canonsburg was dissatisfied with its third baseman he could be sold to some other club in the circuit. And that's what Canonsburg did. Scoops was sold to the Washington (Pennsylvania) team, and while the transaction doesn't entitle him to a place in baseball's Hall of Fame, there ought to be a marker in his honor at a point, say, about twelve miles from Cooperstown. So far as the records show, Scoops was sold for the lowest price ever quoted in the history of such commerce. To get him, Washington paid Canonsburg one two-cent stamp.

EVEN THE BEST of ballplayers has his off days, and Dan O'Leary always remembered that Albany game. In 1878 Dan was a star for the Lowell, Massachusetts, team and he really had an off day in the game with Albany.

176

He gave the York Staters six unearned runs by making errors on two fly balls, each time with the bases full.

At bat he had gone hitless, with Albany players making "impossible" catches of three different line drives.

Albany was well out in front when the ninth inning arrived. Two Lowell batters were retired easily, and then Dan came to the plate. He was determined to redeem himself and when he saw a good pitch coming at him he swung with all his might.

The bat topped the ball, and it dropped to the ground a foot or two in front of the plate. The Lowell catcher dashed forward, grabbed the ball, and was about to fire it down to first when he saw that Dan O'Leary hadn't moved. He was standing there by the plate, disgusted with himself, and now he spoke to the catcher as follows:

"Fer the luvva God, Jim Keenan, touch me with that ball and put an end to this afternoon, the like of which I hope never again finds me drawin' breath."

And Keenan obliged.

THE PRESENTATION of gifts to favorite baseball players has always been a custom among followers of the game. In the early days a star player was often called to home plate and presented with a huge floral wreath or a basket of flowers. There were occasions, however, when unusual gifts came from a player's fans.

First Baseman Isbell of the White Sox, for example, found a celebration awaiting him when he returned to his home town, Wichita, Kansas, in 1906 after his team had won the World Series. The festivities were sponsored by the local plumbers' union (Isbell had once been a plumber), and the gifts had been chosen with an eye to the fact that the White Sox star had grown bald. Among them were a bald eagle and a bald-faced mustang.

A "surprise party" was held at the plate for a Minneapolis player named Werden one day in 1894. Minneapolis was playing Toledo, and the game was a close one until Werden in one of the late innings belted a home run with two men on base. As he came jogging in to home plate, Werden was surprised to see a committee awaiting him. The committee members shook his hand, and then one sedate gentleman delivered a short address paying tribute to Werden as a man four-square, an inspiration to the youth of the land; and finally, on behalf of his multitude of admirers, the committee presented him with an elegant gold watch.

"Gee, thanks!" said Werden. "I really don't know what to say. I really don't."

At last the committee retired, and Werden walked to the bench, a warm glow within him, and sat down. Then he looked at the elegant gold watch and immediately he leaped to his feet and screamed:

"Oh, you sonsabitches!"

The watch that had been presented to him was his own—a watch he had been carrying for five years. It had been given to him in a similar ceremony by his fans in Toledo. Just before the start of the game he had handed his watch, a stickpin, and some money to a friend, asking him to hold it for him until the game was over.

 WHEN THE time came for the National League season of 1887 to begin, members of the Philadelphia Phillies were aglow with pride, for they were to inaugurate the new season and a new ball park at the same time.

A day or two before the opening game was scheduled, however, the Philadelphia manager, by good fortune, wandered out to have a look at the new field. Someone had made a grave error in laying out the diamond. For one thing, the foul lines were much too close together; and there were other technical mistakes, including the fact that second base was crowded up close to the pitcher's mound.

What had happened? The workmen who were sent to lay out the diamond had mistaken the grading stakes for base-line markers.

THE NAME of H. C. Smith should be listed high on the roster of baseball's hero-worshipers.

In the 1890s Smith was station agent for the Chicago & Alton Railroad at the little town of Auburn in Illinois. Another young man who lived at Auburn was Joseph McGinnity, who pitched baseball for the country teams during the week and for Springfield on Sundays. H. C. Smith got to be a great admirer of Joseph McGinnity.

Smith left Auburn in 1895 and went to Chicago, where he entered the brokerage business. Within ten years he was a wealthy man.

Joseph McGinnity, meanwhile, had gone on to greater things and became famous as "Iron Man" McGinnity.

But, as it always does, time caught up with the Iron Man, and the day came when his services were no longer needed. He was given his release by the New York Giants.

Back in Chicago H. C. Smith heard the news. He had never

faltered in his admiration for Joseph McGinnity. It was inconceivable to him that baseball had no further use for his hero. He decided to do something about it. A few days later the newspapers announced that H. C. Smith of Chicago had bought the Newark baseball club of the Eastern League and that Iron Man McGinnity was to be its manager.

 WEATHERLY was playing Laurel Hill one afternoon in 1896 on a field just outside Wilkes-Barre, Pennsylvania.

A shortstop named Blackwell had just made a nice throw to first and was backing up to his fielding position when the ground in front of him began to misbehave. A small hole appeared and grew larger and larger. Shortstop Blackwell turned and ran to the outfield and when he looked back and saw what had happened he fainted. A large part of the diamond had caved in, the field having been laid out above some abandoned mine tunnels, and in the spot where Blackwell had been standing the hole was forty feet deep.

 WILD BILL DONOVAN was pitching for Detroit one day around the beginning of the century. Schmidt was behind the plate. Suddenly Wild Bill was startled to see his catcher flash the signal for a pitchout.

Donovan glanced quickly around to reassure himself that there were no runners on base. Then he shook his head at Schmidt, but again the catcher signaled for a pitchout.

Wild Bill, figuring his catcher was suffering from a momentary lightness in the head, pointed to first base, then to second, then to third—illustrating the glaring fact that no runners were aboard. And still Schmidt called for a pitchout. Now Donovan summoned his catcher to the mound for a conference.

"Listen," Schmidt said to him, "that guy at the plate has been cussin' hell out of Tim Hurst for the way he's been callin' the pitches. So now Tim's mad, and I just heard him tell the guy that no matter where the next pitch is, by God he's gonna call it a strike. That's why I want a real wide one. Throw 'er way out wide, and le's see what happens."

Schmidt went back to the plate and Donovan pitched a ball that was a good three feet outside of the plate.

"Sturrrike!" yelled Umpire Hurst.

The batter shrieked like an agonized emu and then directed some remarks at the umpire, which the umpire adjudged to be passably vile. "Yer outa the game," said Umpire Hurst, and the verdict stood.

SOLOMON, who cut up a baby into chunks or some such thing, was considered to be a wise man. There have been others in the world, and, among them, baseball umpires.

Back in the ancient days of the national pastime an umpire named Hugh Rorty was operating in New England. One afternoon he was officiating at a game between Lynn and Haverhill. Haverhill piled up a fair sort of lead, and when a fog moved over the playing field the Haverhill manager, Bill Luby, concluded it would be nice to have the game called because of bad visibility. Luby, in fact, made quite an argument out of it with Umpire Rorty. When Rorty insisted that the game should continue, Luby stamped his foot in pique and said that doggone it, he oughta know, seeing as how he was the right fielder.

Umpire Rorty turned and picked up a fielding glove.

"Now," he said, "I'm going out to your spot in right. I want you to hit some fungos out there and I'll decide what's what."

Luby hit three towering fungos to right field, and Umpire Rorty galloped back and forth and caught all three of them. Then he came back to the plate and handed the glove to Manager Luby. Play was resumed.

HUNDREDS of Chicago fans were shocked speechless one day in 1916 when they picked up their newspapers and saw a headline which said that Red Faber had been shot and killed.

Faber was a pitching ace of the White Sox. Charles Comiskey, the club owner, was also proprietor of a hunting preserve in Wisconsin. A bad-tempered moose lived on this preserve, and Comiskey called the animal Red Faber. It was the moose, then, that had wandered afield and attacked a farm boy, whose brother then shot the animal.

LARRY LAJOIE was playing first base for Philadelphia one afternoon in New York when a disturbance arose in the stands back of first.

An excited-looking man was running down the aisle, his eyes fixed on Lajoie, and yelling:

"Larry! Larry! Come over here! I've got to talk to you!"

Lajoie, recognizing that the fellow was from his home town of Fall River, Massachusetts, asked the umpire to call time and hurried over to the stand where he and the excited spectator engaged in a brief conversation.

Lajoie was frowning and looked thoroughly unhappy as he returned to his position and signaled that he was ready to resume play. His teammates as well as many spectators who had witnessed the incident figured that Larry had been given some bad news—possibly someone near and dear to him had passed to a greater glory, and everyone concluded that Larry was stoically carrying on, playing the game through to its end though his heart was breaking.

When the inning was over and Lajoie walked slowly to the bench, his fellow players gathered around him and asked him if the man in the grandstand had been a bearer of bad news.

"Yeh," said Lajoie. "When I got over to him, thinking something had happened to my folks, that bum said all he wanted was to borry five dollars so's he could catch the boat back to Fall River. I would of hit him, only it's against the rules."

SOME PEOPLE don't like baseball. Other people don't like baseball parks. Back in 1898 the people who lived in the neighborhood of the old Northwest Baseball Park in Chicago complained regularly about the place, called it an eyesore, a confounded nuisance.

When these complaints failed to bring relief, the unhappy citizens organized a mob. Somehow they managed to borrow a trolley car, which they maneuvered to a position in the street just outside the ball park. Then they attached a cable to a huge timber which helped support the roof of the grandstand and hooked the cable to the streetcar. Clang, clang, clang—and down came the grandstand in splinters. That was the end of the eyesore.

A BUGLER played "Taps" in center field, the flag was gently lowered, and prostitutes wept that day in 1909 when the Pittsburgh Pirates played their last game at the old Exposition Grounds park. The next day Forbes Field was dedicated and became the Pirates' home park.

One of the reasons a new location was chosen and a new park erected was the proximity of Pittsburgh's red-light district to the Exposition Grounds. To reach the old field it was necessary to pass through this sinful area. Consequently the Pittsburgh management was losing out on a growing source of revenue— "decent women" simply refused to pass through Bawdyland to get to the ball games.

WHEN BILLY MURRAY was managing the Phillies in the 1900s, an earnest young bush leaguer joined the club, determined to make good.

In his first game he played acceptable ball for eight innings. In the ninth it came his time to bat. Philadelphia was trailing by a run, two men were out, and there was a runner on third. The rookie got his bat and then stepped over to Manager Murray.

"What do you want me to do?" he asked.

Murray stared at him a moment, then snorted sarcastically, "Strike out."

The rookie walked to the plate, swung listlessly at the first three pitches, and struck out.

By suppertime he was on his way back to the minors.

PETE BROWNING, who played left field for Louisville many years ago, was superstitious. Coming in to the bench from his position in the outfield, he always pursued a course which would permit him to touch third base with his foot.

Pittsburgh was playing Louisville one afternoon. In the fifth inning, just as the third Pittsburgh out was made, one of the Pirates, George Miller, dashed out, pulled third base from its moorings, and carried it back to the bench.

In from left field came Pete Browning, walking with the center fielder. Reaching the point where third base should have been, Pete stuck out his foot, then drew it back and stared in momentary perplexity. He quickly glanced all around the immediate area, then a roar of laughter from the Pittsburgh bench attracted his attention. George Miller was holding the purloined base aloft.

Pete stood there and heard the laughter spread to the stands, and soon the whole park was roaring. Then he got sore. He clenched his fists and started toward Miller.

"Goddamn you!" he yelled. "You put that base back where you got it!"

Miller saw that Pete meant business. Clutching the base to his chest, he leaped from the bench and scampered onto the field. Pete set out after him. The chase lasted several minutes, and Pete was never able to catch up to Miller. At last Miller came running in toward the plate. There he was intercepted by the umpire, who also prevented the angry Pete Browning from braining Miller with a bat.

"That's enough," said the umpire. "Now, go put it back."

Miller dutifully went up the line and re-anchored third base. As soon as it was in place, Pete came up to bat.

The first pitch was a strike, called. The second pitch was a strike, called. Pete held up his hand and then said something to the umpire. The umpire nodded. Pete dropped his bat, ran up the line, touched third base with his foot, then came back to the plate. He hit the next pitch for a sharp single.

SHERWOOD MAGEE, star outfielder for the Philadelphia Nationals in the old days, was the kind of player about whom the fans said, "That guy eats and sleeps baseball."

Magee really loved his job of fielding. One night he had a dream. He was in the field, and a batter had just hit a looping ball that would require some fast running for Magee to get up to it.

Magee fielded the ball through the window of his bedroom and was picked up, not badly hurt, on a tin roof where he had landed. He was ribbed unmercifully by his teammates as well as by the newspapers. A reporter who asked him the cause of the whole affair got this response:

"I et a lot of grapes before I went to bed."

BASEBALL'S CONTRIBUTIONS to the American language have been recognized for many years, and whole books have been written on the subject of baseball slang. The argot, of course, is largely the product of the men who write about the game—not the men who play it. In the earliest days, when a reporter was taken off, say, the supreme court beat and assigned to writing baseball, something queer happened in his head. Not only did he begin inventing words and phrases, but he became among the world's most avid seekers after synonyms.

The early baseball writers, almost to a man, somehow acquired the belief that it would be sinful for them ever to call a base a base, or a ball a ball, or a hit a hit.

So it continued down to our own times, until a routine report on a baseball game became a puzzle in gibberish, resembling an essay written in High Bantu, with dialect. Then something happened, and the whole picture changed so that today it is possible to pick up a newspaper and read the story of a ball game and determine quite readily just what happened.

In 1913 the Philadelphia *Evening Bulletin* grew alarmed at the trend and conducted a symposium on the topic: Should baseball stories be written in straight English or in slang? Among the interesting responses was that of Provost Edgar Fahs Smith of the University of Pennsylvania.

Provost Smith had been a baseball player in his college days, but after he took to provosting he found himself unable to devote the time to attend games. So he tried to keep abreast of things in the newspapers.

"Once or twice," he said, "I have been on the verge of clipping the story of a ball game and sending it to the office in which it was published, together with a request for a translation or interpretation. Baseball is a wonderful game, and it is a pity that the pleasure of reading about it should be spoiled. It seems to me as if the baseball reporters were being paid to hide the truth about the game by use of strange verbiage, instead of to set it forth."

We could fill this book with examples of remarkable baseball writing, taken from old newspaper files. Let it suffice that a couple of samples be presented, both chosen at random.

Here is a paragraph from a story written in 1887:

> Tiernan was lucky enough to get first base on balls. Just as he started to burglarize the second hassock, Ward smote the ball furiously to right center. Tiernan ran all the way home with New York's first run of the game. Then there was a cheer, and a gamin on the bleaching boards cried, "Hooray! We ain't skunked!"

A sports writer in Lowell, Massachusetts, committed the following in 1883:

> He lay in a swoon by the roadside. His helmet was broken, his visor was cracked, his gorget was tarnished with the smoke of battle, his breast-plate was indented like a milk can, his halberd was as dull as a five-cent barber's razor, the lock of his cross gun was shattered, his arquebus was shivered, his quiver shook like a canal horse with the heaves, his tabard was in shreds, his ears were gone, one eye was missing, his nose was out of plumb, and his jawbone was paralyzed. He had been trying to umpire.

Back in 1909 the New York *Sun* chose to poke fun at the Chicago *Tribune* for the fanciful prose of its sports writers. Among the sample sentences mentioned were:

> The Cardinals were outbatted by many parasangs.

188

Jeff Overall cut the cardiac region of the plate.

But for Brown's unfortunate decease, he could have scored standing up.

GOAT ANDERSON'S position on the roster of the Pittsburgh Pirates was none too secure when the rookie reported to the team's spring training camp. In an exhibition game, Anderson flubbed a signal. When he came in from the field Manager Fred Clarke was waiting for him and launched into the customary dressing down reserved for clumsy bushers. The veteran manager had just begun to apply the heavy sarcasm when Anderson interrupted.

"Ah, shut up!" said the rookie. "You don't know everything!"

His astounded teammates stepped back, expecting action, figuring Manager Clarke would at least pick up the boy and throw him over the fence. No such thing happened. Clarke stared at the rookie for a long time and then spoke.

"Son," he said, "you got spirit. I like you."

And Goat Anderson landed a job with the Pirates.

THE QUESTION of Sunday baseball plagued the town of Hartford City, Indiana, in 1905. A group of businessmen had organized and financed a baseball team as a civic enterprise. They felt that they would be unable to make a go of the thing unless Sunday games were

permitted, yet the pressure against Sunday baseball was powerful, coming mainly from a local theological seminary. At last
one of the businessmen found the solution. He proposed that a
local clergyman be invited to preach a sermon at the ball park
just before the start of each Sunday game and that when the
last amen had been uttered, the cry of "play ball!" would be
permitted.

The idea was accepted. So throughout that season the fans
arrived early at the ball park. When they had assembled, a
clergyman took his place at home plate and sassed Satan for a
half hour or so—never once alluding to the evil of Sunday
baseball. As soon as he finished, the ball game started.

DURING the 1920s there was a definite pattern
widely popular among writers who were producing
slick baseball fiction. Short stories with a baseball
background usually were fashioned around the eccentricity of a
single player.

This central character was either mentally deficient in one
way or another or possessed some physical abnormality; whatever the flaw in his make-up may have been, it served as the
gimmick for tangling the plot and then untangling it.

The old newspaper files contain a short piece of baseball
fiction which may have been the grandpappy of all the short
stories in this category. It is the tale of Lampless Lewis and it
appeared in the New York *Sun* back in 1903. For its historical
value and because it is amusing, we would like to reprint it
almost in full.

The tale is narrated by an ex-mascot who is trying to illus-
trate the magnetic attraction of baseball, how "when a man gets
really to know the game thoroughly, there's nothing on earth

will make him lose his interest in it." He recalls the case of Lampless Lewis, who played with the Lightfoot Lillies.

In the middle of his career Lewis went stone blind, yet he refused to give up baseball.

"I mean," said the ex-mascot, "he went right on playing left field for the Lightfoot Lillies. And I'll have you understand, sir, that there wasn't a finer outfielder in the business. . . .

"Well, anyhow, some jealous woman who'd mistaken him for another guy gave him the carbolic sling one day, and he lost the use of both peepers. Now, you'd naturally think that would have meant his finish as a ballplayer; but it didn't.

"Have you ever noticed how when a man loses the use of a leg or something, the strength that was in that leg always goes to some other part of his body? Why, take some of these skinny armless little guys you see; they have underpinnings on them that Samson needn't have been ashamed of before he had his hair out.

"Well, that's the way it was with Lewis. When he lost his eyesight it went to his nose. He developed a sense of smell that would have brought tears of envy to the eyes of the finest bloodhounds that ever sniffed a scent.

"We discovered this at practice one day. Lewis was standing close by, listening to the batting, when a wild pitch made straight for him.

" 'Look out!' we yelled.

"But Lewis, to our amazement, instead of dodging, threw up his dukes and gobbled the ball in as easy as you please.

" 'I thought I smelled 'er coming,' he explained. 'Violets, isn't it?' he added with a sniff.

"We couldn't figure out what he meant until Bull Thompson, shamefaced and blushing, admitted that he had washed his hands with scented soap that morning. A slight perfume had clung to the ball, and Lewis had smelled out its course.

" 'By the great Dan Brouthers!' exclaimed Slugger Burrows

enthusiastically. 'There's no reason why you should give up baseball, Lewis. Report for practice in your old place in left tomorrow.'

"Lewis did report; and say, would you believe it, he was as good a fielder as he ever had been before his accident. A single drop of heliotrope placed on the ball in the first inning was enough to make him follow it around like a hound all the rest of the game.

"At the bat he was even better than he had been before. His keen sense of smell enabled him to tell which way the ball was twisting the minute it left the pitcher's hand, and he always knew exactly what curve to expect.

"The one thing that troubled us about Lewis for a time was his base running. We first tried spraying heliotrope along the base line. That would work all right for a few innings, but after the ball had been batted around the diamond some he was likely to run afoul of grounder trails. When he did, he was just as apt as not to leave his course suddenly and dart out to center field on some false scent.

"It was Bull Thompson who finally solved the problem. While we still stuck to heliotrope for the ball perfume, we substituted a powerful essence of white rose as a base-line spray. This worked to perfection and, save for a few days when he had a slight cold in the head, there wasn't a better base runner on the team than Lampless Lewis.

"But, like most great men, Lewis had his downfall. And, as luck would have it, it came just when it would be most felt.

"It was in the last inning of the great contest with the Ringtail Roarers for the championship of Jones County. The Lillies were leading, 12 to 10, and had the bases full, with two men out.

"On the third ball pitched the batter drove a long fly to left. We started to put on our hats. Lew's nose had never failed us.

"But this time the unexpected happened. Just as Lewis was

stretching forth his hands to receive the ball, some well-meaning admirer in the bleachers threw a bouquet at him.

"An agonizing expression of indecision came over Lewis's face. He hesitated. The pungent perfume of the freshly picked flowers was too much for him. He dived wildly at the flying bouquet, the men on bases cantered home, and the game was lost.

"But that wasn't all. The ball struck Lewis on the nose and broke it. His stock in trade as a baseball player was ruined for ever afterward."

 MEMPHIS was playing at Mobile one day in 1914 when a heavy fog moved in from the gulf. One of the Memphis batters met the ball squarely, and it disappeared into the vapors hanging over the field. What happened to the ball after that remains a mystery—it was never found anywhere on the playing field, so the assumption was that it went over the fence. The umpire called it a home run.

On the outfield fences were the customary advertising signs, including these:

HIT ONE OVER THIS SIGN
AND GET A SUIT OF CLOTHES.

KNOCK IT OVER THE FENCE HERE
AND GET A QUART OF WHISKY.

GET A HOMER ABOVE THIS SIGN
AND COLLECT A DOZEN PAIRS OF SOX.

The Memphis man whose hit had disappeared in the fog made the rounds of the local merchants the next morning, collecting a suit of clothes, two bottles of liquor, a dozen socks, a hat, and two pounds of coffee. "It *could* of gone over your sign," he told each merchant, and nobody gave him an argument.

SEVENTY YEARS AGO the Philadelphia Athletics played a game at Pottsville, Pennsylvania, on a field which the "city fellers" said was a caution. The outfield sloped so steeply that the three fielders could not be seen by the spectators or the scorekeeper. Moreover, the right-field fence was so close in that Al Reach hit the ball over it four times in a row. The score of the contest was: Philadelphia, 107; Pottsville, 2. Sports writers said the most noteworthy feature of the game was Foran's performance. He was at bat so many times in the early part of the game that he was put out three times in the first inning and twice in the second, actually making the first five outs.

A DEVICE known as a "German Disturber" was fairly common in baseball contests during the 1880s. It consisted of a keg of beer and a dipper, located alongside third base. Any player who reached that base was entitled to a dipperful of beer. The social tone of such contests is suggested in the New York *Clipper's* account of a game between Bridgeport and New Haven, sponsored by the Bridgeport Elks Club in 1888. Said the *Clipper*:

> The game was a big success, but not tiresome. The good players made

just enough errors and the poor players just enough good plays to make the contest interesting. The way both teams ran bases would make the St. Louis Browns and the Chicagos turn green with envy.

Killingbeck was the first man to reach the German Disturber on third base after getting a single and going to third on another single. He waved the dipper aloft and drank to the success of his team. Rocket was so engaged with the keg when he reached third in the second inning that he would not start for the plate when the next batter slammed a long hit. Simmons, getting tired of staying on second and thinking more of scoring than making a stop at the keg, ran past Rocket and scored. That was voted the most brilliant play of the game, even though it was contrary to the rules.

Brother Charles Daniels umpired. Music was furnished by Prof. Mazziotta and Wagner's Garden Band. At seven-thirty all hands sat down to a shore dinner. Result of the ball game: Bridgeport, 18; New Haven, 14.

TRAVELING through the South in the spring of 1896, the Cincinnati Reds arrived in New Orleans for a game with the local club. A great throng turned out for the contest, and the Cincinnati manager, feeling that his team was so superior that the game would probably be a dull one, decided to handicap the New Orleans club. They were given four outs in each inning to three for Cincinnati. It was a fair job of handicapping—Cincinnati won in the late innings by a score of 9 to 7.

 IN HIS GREAT DAYS Tim Hurst kept an uncivil tongue in his head. When he excoriated a player, that player stayed excoriated for quite some time. Among all the colorful umpires that the game has seen, Tim was the most skilled in the uses of biting sarcasm.

Yet as he neared the end of his career Tim appeared to be mellowing. Instead of blistering players with his tongue, he often spoke to them gently, in a friendly manner, and, considering his past performances, this was a marvel to behold.

"Jimminy cripes!" said the fans. "Looka ole Tim Hurst a-bein' perlite!"

For years Tim had carried on a feud with Kid Elberfield, the harum-scarum infielder for the New York Highlanders. Elberfield was called "The Tabasco Kid" because of his violent temper, and it was inevitable that he and Tim Hurst would be almost constantly at loggerheads.

Then came the mellowing of Hurst, and one day in 1906 he astounded even himself by engaging in a pleasant conversation with Kid Elberfield. He even found himself giving some well-intentioned paternal advice to The Tabasco Kid.

"Kid," he said, "you're being a damn fool whenever you cuss an empire. All you've ever got for it has been a long string of fines and suspensions. I'm gonna give you a little advice. Let Clark Griffith do the fighting for the club. He gets the big salary for running the team. Let him take the jolts."

"But," interposed Elberfield, "I'm the team captain, and it's up to me to look out for the team's interest and raise the devil when you umpires don't treat us good. I think you're wrong."

All the mellowness went out of Tim Hurst now. The old acid returned. This squirt—giving him an argument!

"Lord help us!" he exclaimed. "You—or the likes of you—being captain of a big-league ball team! What a laugh! The management ought to be fined a thousand dollars for even letting you on the field, you pint-sized pipsqueak!"

Elberfield just smiled. He knew that Tim Hurst was back in form.

THERE WAS a day in 1884 when, if you had been in Quincy, Illinois, and you had asked someone the whereabouts of the local baseball team, you probably would have been told, "Oh, they're being given a tryout down to St. Louis today."

The Quincy team had withdrawn from the Northwestern League in a dispute of some kind and then had applied for admission to the Union Association, a league that had just recently been organized.

The boss men of the Quincy team went down to St. Louis to lay their case before officials of the Union Association, only to find that the new league was not overly anxious to take Quincy in. The league officials didn't think the Quincy team was sharp enough to travel in their company.

"Look," said one of the Quincy men, "your teams try out individual players to see if they're good enough to be signed. Why can't the Association try out a whole team?"

Thus it came about that a "tryout" game was scheduled between Quincy and the St. Louis unions. A Mr. Sweeney pitched for St. Louis, and Quincy was held to two hits, with St. Louis winning handily. Quincy was rejected for league membership but got a good deal of satisfaction out of the fact that, a week or so later, the Union Association folded—a financial failure.

THE BUSINESS of stalling in baseball in an effort to achieve victory has furnished hot-stove leaguers with many a tale to tell, but none goofier than the story of the Philadelphia-Pittsburgh game at Philadelphia in June of 1906.

Going into the eighth inning, Philadelphia was ahead 1 to 0. As Pittsburgh came to bat, rain began falling and low clouds darkened the field. The Philadelphia players urged Umpire Bill Klem to call the game. Klem waved them to their positions afield. A contemporary newspaper account takes up the story from that point:

> Doolin fumbled Beaumont's grounders. Courtney missed Ganley's sacrifice bunt, and a wild pitch advanced both men. They both scored on hits by Clarke and Wagner. Nealon was hit by the pitcher, and Gleason fumbled Lynch's grounders. Ritchey hit to right center, and Thomas made no effort to field the ball. Titus relayed the ball to Doolin, who threw it into the stands, clearing the bases.
>
> To defeat the Phillies' purpose of having the game called back to the preceding inning because of the

storm, the Pirates hastened their play, trying intentionally to be put out and have their side retired. Phelps struck out intentionally, and Willis attempted to do likewise, but Pittinger, the Philly pitcher, hit him in the ribs with the ball, putting him on base. Pittinger then made a wild pitch, but Willis remained on first base. Umpire Klem then benched Pittinger. Both Ward and Thomas then attempted to pitch, but Klem refused to let them make a further farce of the game.

Pitcher McCloskey then came leisurely from the clubhouse, pitched three warm-up balls, and was ordered out of the festivities by Umpire Klem. Lush then went to the mound and repeated McCloskey's tactics of lazily tossing warm-up pitches, although warned by the umpire. After Lush, pitching to the batters, had made several wild pitches, Klem forfeited the game to Pittsburgh and was escorted off the field by police, amid a great heaving of cushions by the fans. A few moments later the storm broke loose with a heavy downpour of rain, and that probably saved the umpire from violence.

HAL CHASE, widely regarded as the best first baseman in the majors during the beginning years of this century, put in a hurry call one morning for a doctor. He had a splinter in his tongue.

The doctor removed the sliver of wood and then went on his way. Apparently he talked about the unusual nature of the case. In any case, the story of how Chase happened to get a splinter in his tongue was soon in general circulation. Hal Chase was a bat-biter. He bit bats, so the story went, for the purpose of testing the quality of the wood in them.

There were, of course, a great many people who figured it was just another wild story and refused to believe it. But verification of a sort came when a sports writer sought out the mascot of the New York Americans (Chase's team) and asked the boy about it.

"Yes, sir," said the mascot, "it's true. Almost every bat we have around our bench has got Mr. Chase's teeth marks on it. He just sorta gnaws on them."

"How," asked the sports writer, "can he tell anything about a bat by biting it?"

"Mr. Chase," responded the mascot, "never lets anybody know what he finds out by biting the bats."

THE MOST remarkable baseball story of the 1893 season concerned the activities of the Mitten League, which was composed of eight teams. Its players all wore heavy deerskin mittens, earmuffs, and fur coats. Even the pitchers wore the thick and cumbersome mittens on their throwing hands.

The Mitten League was organized in the Arctic Circle. The eight teams were called the Hoodlums, the Walruses, the Roaring Gimlets, the Auroras, the Blubbers, the Fat Men, the Invincibles, and the Captains.

The players were officers and men from whaling vessels

which were frozen in at Herschel Island. The playing fields were laid out on the ice.

The Mitten Leaguers had to adapt their style of play, of course, to the conditions under which they were operating. Sliding for a base was much more popular than in ball games back home. For example, a man starting from first for second would take only about half-a-dozen steps, then throw himself onto the ice and scoot three fourths of the distance to reach the bag. There was another distinct difference: the outfielders had the toughest job of anybody on the field. When a line drive was hit, unless the fielder got in front of it and stopped it, the ball very likely would travel a mile and a half. This problem was partly solved eventually by erecting snowbanks at a reasonable distance in the outfield.

The whaling ships were frozen in again the following winter, but attempts to renew Mitten League competition failed. Most of the men simply said it was "too durn much work."

STRONG DRINK was a far greater problem among baseball players of yesteryear than it is today. During the season of 1888 a baseball writer for the Detroit *Free Press* covered a series between Detroit and the Giants. One article which he produced deserves reprinting here for the reason that it sheds light on the off-field activities of the players of that period and for the additional reason that it is a nice job, considering that it was produced in the Cro-Magnon era of sports writing. It follows:

> When one takes into consideration the delicate constitutions and sensitiveness to weather and other malev-

olent influences of the players of the New York Club, one is filled with deepest admiration for the pluck displayed by the invalids in their struggle for the pennant. To see them on the field gives the impression that they had indeed sprung from a race of giants and possessed the toughness of lignum vitae. One would never suppose that the gigantic Connor, the sturdy O'Rourke, the wiry and smiling Welch, and the rest of the sun-browned band were other than a collection of hardy athletes. Appearances in this instance are very deceiving, and those rugged exteriors and smiling fronts mask a collection of ills that would make short work of ordinary mortals. All ballplayers suffer more or less from injuries during their play, and the New Yorks are no exception. When, in addition to this, it is known that each of the Giants is afflicted with an insidious complaint that is liable to prostrate him at any moment, their courageous conduct rises to the level of heroism. Hardly a game is played by the Giants but one of their number succumbs to his particular affliction and is carried to his hotel on a stretcher. An adequate idea of the deplorable condition of the Giants was furnished yesterday at the Hotel Cadillac, where they are stopping. Jim Mutrie rushed madly downstairs yesterday morning and gave a ring on the telephone that caused all the girls in the central office to utter a suppressed scream.

"Give me number ——!" screeched Jim.

"Is this Doctor ——?" he yelled as soon as the connection was made. On an affirmative reply being made he continued:

"Doctor, come to the Cadillac as quick as you can. Roger Connor is down with nervous prostration, and I'm afraid he won't be able to play today. Doctor, you must tone up his shattered nerves. So get over here with a slide."

The physician brought some Moxie over for Roger and departed. Hardly had the son of Esculapius reached his office when there was a ring at the telephone and Mutrie besought him to hurry back to the hotel, as O'Rourke was threatened with palpitation of the heart. The doctor gave James an ounce of prevention and once more sought his office. In a very short time the anguished tones of Mutrie came floating over the phone, informing the physician that Mickey Welch, right in the midst of one of his happiest smiles, had been attacked with faceache, and it was doubtful if he could live through the day. The doctor prescribed a smile antidote for Mickey, pocketed his third fee, and went on his way rejoicing. Before long he was recalled by Mutrie, who imparted the tearful intelligence that Buck Ewing must have inflammation of the brain. At any rate, Buck's head was swelled to twice its natural size and needed attending to at once.

The physician ordered copious applications of congealed *aqua pura* and again withdrew. But he was called back at short intervals during the day to look after various members of the team who were attacked with deadly complaints, and his efforts resulted in the unfortunate men being able to take a bus to Recreation Park in the afternoon. The only one who had not complained of illness that morning was Murphy, and Mutrie was happy because Murphy was down to catch Keefe. The wiry little catcher jumped around in the preliminary practice lively as a cricket and apparently was in robust health. In the first inning he had some difficulty in guessing where Keefe's curves were going to land, and a passed ball by Murphy gave the Detroits their first run. When it was Murphy's turn to go to bat, a sturdy young man named Foster stepped to the plate. Hanlon wanted to know the wherefore, and then the sad intelligence was spread that poor Murphy had been stricken with sudden illness. What it was no one could tell, but it was some virulent disorder that was liable to cut him off in the flower of his youth. He sat on the platform back of the players' bench with a deathly pallor on his countenance. After a protest the change was permitted, and in the next inning O'Rourke went behind the bat and Foster went to left field.

When Manager Leadley thinks the Detroits have sufficiently distinguished themselves in the preliminary practice, he seizes a bell rope that dangles from the grandstand and clangs the brass four times. This is the signal for the game to begin, and at this point the umpire walks out on the diamond. Mr. Kelly's white uniform did not make its appearance yesterday when the signal was given. . . . Kelly's non-appearance is not hard to explain. The man who has masqueraded as a star umpire has for some time past been attempting the difficult feat of rendering proper decisions on the ball field and at the same time maintaining intimate relations with an extensive "jag."

JOHN (STUFFY) McINNIS, who played first for the Athletics years ago, was a man of distinction in baseball, but to his own way of thinking his favorite achievement was the home run he once hit while all of the fielders had their backs turned to him.

Philadelphia was playing at Boston in 1911, and McInnis was scheduled to be first man at bat in the top of the eighth. The Boston pitcher, Karger, was on the mound, and Nunamaker was catching. These two men had reached their positions, McInnis was standing at the plate with bat in hand, but the remaining members of the Boston team were taking their time about getting onto the field. It was a hot day, and the fielders were walking listlessly toward their positions when Karger decided to throw down a few warm-up pitches.

He had forgotten that, a short time before, President Ban

Johnson of the American League had issued an order forbidding warm-up pitches between innings on the grounds that such procedure slowed up the game. So Karger threw one pitch and then wound up for another, and as the ball came in Stuffy McInnis belted it. Not one of the Boston fielders had reached his position and the ball went over their heads and rolled to the fence. No one retrieved it immediately, such was the surprise, but McInnis scampered merrily around the bases and crossed the plate. A great rhubarb ensued, but Umpire Egan ruled that the pitch had been a legal one, that McInnis had every right to swing on it, and that the home run counted.

NO BASEBALL PLAYER in history was ever more cantankerous toward umpires than John J. McGraw when he was at Baltimore. His all-around orneriness was as much a part of his fame as his ability on the field. Yet he was able to retain his sense of humor.

In 1899 President Young of the National League got to talking about McGraw's eternal war with the umpires. Mr. Young said that during the playing season he received a letter from McGraw every two or three days. It usually went like this:

> *Dear Mr. Young:*
> Enclosed please find five dollars which I pay for the privilege of calling one of your umpires a stiff. I think he was a stiff on this particular occasion, but we all have our faults. Please acknowledge receipt and oblige. Kindly offer my regards to the umpire in question, who compelled me to separate with the enclosed five spot.
> Sincerely,
> *John J. McGraw*

DETROIT won the National League pennant in 1887 while the St. Louis Browns emerged as champions of the American Association. There was no such thing as a World Series in that period, but the two pennant winners went on tour together, playing a series of fifteen games to decide which team was "champion of champions."

The excitement attending the series, especially when the two teams arrived in New York, is reflected in a newspaper account which follows in part:

The confusion at 110th Street and Third Avenue approached bedlam. Like lunatics on parade, a large colony of cabdrivers tussled, tugged, and yelled, quite drowning the roar of the arriving cars.

"Fifteen cents to the Polo Grounds!"

"Here's your downy carriage, sir!"

"This way for velvet cushions and race horses!"

The elevated trains came rushing in quick succession, packed to the guards. For a long hour Sixth Avenue and Third Avenue continued to bring thousand after thousand. It was a great day, the day when the champions of the league and those of the association were to meet in flannel armor and contest the palm before the critical eyes of the biggest baseball village in America.

The crowd gathered rapidly. At two o'clock they began to come on foot and in hack loads. The hackmen rode on the horses. There were five men on the back seat and five on the front seat, five standing up, four on the driver's seat, three in front of it, and several underneath.

They poured through the turnstiles in long and steady streams. Like a human freshet they overflowed the grandstand, the special stand, and all the standing room. Ladies were numerous. Their bonnets glistened and their ribbons fluttered.

The field was a pretty picture. The bright green grass stretched prettily over the field, level as a billiard table.

Outside in the street the telegraph poles were cluttered with men who chose that vantage point rather than pay fifty cents for admission. New York's population gathered to the number of ten thousand.

At two o'clock the players arrived. Two hacks came first, laden with nine stalwart men in white caps. The crowd made a rush and surrounded the carriages which bore the Detroit team. They had to step on small boys to reach the ground, and the small boys were proud of being stepped on. Then they doffed their coats and quietly went to work, banging the white bullet at each other with deadly certainty.

The St. Louis team arrived in more carriages and received more cheers and admiration. No debutantes or prima donnas ever were more closely inspected than were the nine in blue and brown. They were a trifle gaudy as they descended with scarlet blazers over their bright blue uniforms. They, too, fell to practicing.

The Detroit men are a much finer-looking lot, both muscularly and facially. Baseball, like race riding, has come to be quite as much a matter of brains as of muscle, and the Detroits appeared to have a marked advantage in intellectual equipment. They appeared to be older men, too, and went about their work more seriously. When the game started they began hammering the ball without loss of time. When they went out with three runs to their credit, the faces of the St. Louis players were as blue as their uniforms.

In the second inning of the Browns there was a slight interruption. Bennett, the catcher of the Detroits, had split his finger. It did not seem to be anything unusual for either Bennett or his fingers. When he held up that battered right hand with the fingers swollen and spread like a boxing glove, with rags tied around three of them, and the entire hand having the general appearance of having been run over by a freight car, it did not seem as though there was room to split it in any new place. He went right on with his play. The ball came in from Getsein like a shot, whizzing and curving. But the catcher grabbed it surely and deftly, though the blood was reddening his hand and could be seen now and then dripping to the ground. . . .

During the game Superintendent Curtis accidentally shot himself in the hand while exhibiting a new revolver to a friend seated beside him in the stand. As usual, he didn't know it was loaded. He was taken to a hospital, where his wound was dressed.

Sticklers for statistics, who might want to know how the game and the series came out, are hereby informed that the "intellectual equipment" and over-all beauty of the Detroits triumphed in both.

 IN THE vast body of baseball legend the name of Wilbert Robinson occupies a special position. Scores of flavorsome tales have him for protagonist. Most of the Robinson stories are familiar to the dyed-in-the-wool fan and therefore have no place in this book. There is one little incident, however, which turned up in the old newspaper files, and which we feel will bear repeating.

One afternoon, just before his Brooklyn Dodgers were to take the field, Uncle Robbie sat on the bench with pencil and paper, getting his starting line-up written down for the plate umpire.

Someone observed that, after writing down three or four names, a worrisome hesitation overtook the fabulous Brooklyn manager. He glanced around as though for help and then spoke to a player who was sitting near him. The player shrugged and shook his head. Uncle Robbie then resumed his writing. The nature of the perplexity that had come upon him was brought to light later in the day.

In writing down the line-up, Uncle Robbie had arrived at one of the outfield positions, where he wanted to play Oscar Roettger. He started to write Oscar's name, then realized that he had no idea how to spell "Roettger." Turning to the player nearest him, he asked:

"How the devil do you spell Oscar's last name?"

The player didn't know. So Uncle Robbie wrote down "Cox." And Dick Cox played right field that afternoon in place of Oscar Roettger.

MANAGER WILLIAM JOYCE of the New York Giants had reason to be in a bad humor one September afternoon in 1898 at Washington. At the end of the sixth inning the score was 12 to 1 in favor of Washington, and there was more grief ahead. When the Giants came to bat in the seventh, Warner was called out at first on a close play and got into a loud and profane dispute with Umpire Connolly, who soon banished him. By this time Manager Joyce had completely lost control of himself. He screamed and bellowed and hopped up and down in his rage, only to be laughed at and taunted by the Washington fans.

The spectators hooted him as he took his place at third base, yelling splendid sarcasms at him. That only served to aggravate him, and finally he reached such a state of anger that he yelled:

"By God, if they want somethin' to laugh at, I'll give 'em somethin' to laugh at!"

He called for time and then began shouting orders to his

players. He told Second Baseman Gleason to play first. He shifted Doyle, the first baseman, to second. Doheny, a pitcher, was stationed at third. Van Haltran came in from center field to play shortstop. Gettig, the right fielder, was brought in to pitch, and Seymour, who had been pitching, was told to go behind the plate and catch.

"Then," said a newspaper account of the mess, "began an exhibition of farcical baseball that will stand for years as a disgrace against the men who participated. Man after man would come to bat for Washington, hit the ball, and run the bases at will. All that time the misfits were making fools of themselves and throwing the ball around the lot. Umpire Connolly came to the rescue and put an end to the disgraceful scene by shouting that the game had been officially concluded with the end of the sixth inning and that there would be no more action on the diamond that day."

 THE STORY of Casey Stengel and the sparrow has been told in many variations. Usually it is warped around so that it becomes a piece of deliberate screwball behavior on the part of Stengel. Newspaper accounts of the incident, written in 1918 right after it occurred, would seem to contradict these versions.

Stengel was a great hero in the few years he played with the Dodgers; then he was traded to the Pirates. On that day in 1918 he came back to Brooklyn as a member of the Pittsburgh club. Technically he had now gone over to the enemy, yet the Brooklyn fans held him in such high esteem that it was a sure thing they would salute him with cheers on his return.

He did not bat in the top of the first, but was the first man scheduled to hit for Pittsburgh at the beginning of the second. He walked out of the dugout when the time came, selected a bat, and strode to the plate. The Brooklyn fans got to their feet and cheered him mightily. Arriving at the plate, Casey turned and faced the stands and lifted his cap from his head in acknowledgment of the salute, and a bird flew out of his hair, circled the diamond once, and then disappeared into the sky. A great roar went up from the multitude—old Casey hadn't disappointed 'em!

The fact appears to be that Mr. Stengel was as greatly startled as the fans had been when a bird flew out of his thatch. For the moment, however, he made no effort to disillusion his admirers, being content to let them think he had rigged the bird trick in their honor.

Later on he told his story of what had happened. When he had gone to his position in right field in the first inning, he saw an injured sparrow wobbling along at the base of the wall. He walked over and picked it up and was trying to decide what to do with it when he noticed that the ball game had been resumed and he needed to get down to business. He quickly placed the stunned bird under his cap and went to work as an outfielder. He swore later on that he had completely forgotten about the sparrow when he came in from the field and went to bat. Nonetheless, the bird story has been widely repeated as an example of Stengel's showmanship.

JOHN J. McGRAW, during the time when he was known as "Muggsy" and brought sleepless nights to many an umpire, was usually explosive and violent on the playing field. But he could also be beguiling.

One day in 1894, at Baltimore, McGraw came to bat with Orioles on first and second. He bunted down the first-base line. The pitcher, Red Ehret, scampered over to field the ball. He was just reaching for it when it disappeared. McGraw, charging down the line toward first, had kicked the ball, booting it into right field.

The base runners, including Muggsy, hurried on their way. Two of them had scored, and McGraw himself came on around third and headed for home plate. Red Ehret was standing near the plate, watching McGraw and laughing fit to kill— he was certain that Umpire Betts would call everybody out and maybe even throw McGraw out of the park.

Muggsy McGraw apparently anticipated the same thing, for he came steaming into the plate, touched it, then turned quickly to the umpire and said:

"Didn't kick it on purpose. Honest! Cross my heart!"

And Umpire Betts believed him—ruling all three runs were legal.

ON AUGUST 19, 1909, the New York American League baseball team crossed the Hudson and that afternoon played a nine-inning contest with the Jersey City team of the Eastern League.

It was a most peculiar affair. No band played. The fielders for each team went about their work soundlessly, without the customary chatter. And, most remarkable of all, the crowded stands and bleachers were almost as still as the desert at midnight. Base hits were made, but no spectator cheered or jeered or even clapped his hands. The umpires rendered questionable decisions, yet no one screamed at them in anger. Peanut and soft-drink peddlers moved through the crowd, but no huckster cries came from them. Save for the occasional noise made when the bat met the ball or 'when the ball met a glove, it was a game played in astonishing silence.

There was a reason. The silent game was played on a Sunday afternoon. The New York team had crossed to Jersey because New York City had a law which forbade ball games on Sunday. At the same time, legislation aimed against Sunday ball games was pending in the Jersey courts. There was a strong possibility that the Jersey authorities would step in, once the contest had started, and serve some warrants.

So the management devised a scheme to avoid trouble, if possible. Each spectator as he entered the park was handed a printed card urging him to keep his big mouth shut throughout the afternoon. He was told why and he was told that if he yelled or even clapped his hands the law might descend on the park. It seems an amazing thing, but newspaper reports say the fans obeyed the injunction to a man and that a person passing near the park that afternoon would never have known that a baseball game was in progress.

In those times there was an almost constant ruckus over Sunday baseball, and raids by the authorities were nearly as common as assaults upon umpires. It actually got so that a special stratagem was developed by managers—whenever there was the slightest chance of a raid, the lead-off hitter in the top of the first inning was always a lowly substitute player. When the cops arrived it was their custom to arrest everyone in the immediate vicinity of home plate, meaning the catcher, the umpire, and the batter. By sending a second-string player to bat, a manager made certain that he would not lose the services of a regular through arrest.

The Jersey City affair was the only one, so far as is known, in which the device of sepulchral silence was used to circumvent the law. Other teams tried other methods. In Brooklyn,

for example, back in 1905 the law didn't actually forbid baseball games—it forbade the charging of admission to games on
Sunday. So the Brooklyn management on an April Sunday
that year found a way to get around the statute. Fans arriving
at Washington Park had to buy score cards before they were
admitted. They paid anywhere from twenty-five cents to a dollar for the cards, depending on where they wanted to sit. The
cops were present in force, but they took no action while 11,642
fans bought their score cards and walked to their seats.

There were other instances where "contribution boxes" were
installed at the entrances to ball parks, and the fans were
trusted to drop their proper donations through the slots before
taking their seats.

 LOCAL AUTHORITIES in Provincetown, Massachusetts, were dead set against Sunday baseball
back in 1906. They didn't want any Sunday baseball of any kind played in their community. They knew that
the North Atlantic Fleet of the United States Navy would, as
usual, put in at Provincetown during the summer; and they
knew that it was a custom among the sailors, when they came
ashore, to organize a ball game. So they rigged up a petition and
sent it to the Navy Department, requesting that an official order be issued, forbidding any baseball in Provincetown.

The petition finally reached the hands of Rear Admiral
Evans, who was in charge of the fleet maneuvers. Admiral
Evans gave it but a moment's consideration, then announced
that Provincetown was being removed from the fleet's itiner-
ary—not only for that year but for future years.

When this intelligence reached Provincetown there was a

great hullabaloo, and an emergency meeting of selectmen was called, and various speakers said their pieces. The selectmen then agreed that they had been hasty and, in effect, announced that the sailors could play Sunday baseball up and down the main street if they felt like it.

CINCINNATI was playing at Philadelphia one September afternoon in 1900 when Tommy Corcoran, the third-base coach for the visitors, suddenly appeared to have gone mad.

Corcoran let out a whoop, dropped to his knees, and began digging furiously in the manner of a dog excavating for a bone.

Players and policemen rushed over to find out what had happened to Corcoran, but he brushed them aside and in a moment pulled a board out of the hole he had been digging. Beneath the board was a small pit, and from this hole Corcoran now dragged some kind of mechanical contrivance fitted out with wires.

Thus began a scandal which kept the baseball circuits gabbing for months. Cincinnati contended that Philadelphia had installed an elaborate electrical system which was employed in stealing signals from opposing teams. Manager Bob Allen of the Cincinnati club said that Morgan Murphy, a spare catcher for the Phillies, during each game sat in a window of the clubhouse, which was out in center field. Murphy had field glasses which he used to detect the signals of the opposing catcher. He then transmitted certain impulses to the box concealed beneath the third-base coaching line. The coach at third base always kept one foot directly above the gadget, and he could feel "vibrathrobs" with that foot. Receiving the vibrathrobs from Murphy, the coach would quickly signal the Philadelphia man at bat, and the batter would know immediately what kind of pitch to anticipate.

The Cincinnati manager charged that Philadelphia had been winning games regularly through the use of this nefarious device—pointing out that the Phillies had been eminently successful on their home grounds whereas they were consistent losers on the road.

The Philadelphia management denied everything. The hidden box was not for signaling at all—it was something left over from a carnival company which had occupied the grounds for a few weeks—part of the lighting system.

Discovery of the Philadelphia vibrathrob device touched off a whole series of charges and countercharges involving signal stealing. Scarcely a game went by without someone emitting a howl and accusing someone else of employing illegal methods to steal signals.

Some of these charges apparently were true. One of the most common contrivances turned up was the "sentry-box" system. A shanty or lean-to would be erected against the outside of the fence, usually in center field. The chief signal stealer would enter this "sentry box" before the start of a game and through a hole in the fence train his binoculars on the catcher. His method of signaling to the batter usually involved a portion of the advertising sign painted on the fence at the point where he was operating.

For example, the "sentry-box" system discovered one day on the grounds of the New York Americans employed the billboard ad of a New York hatter. The man in the box outside the fence used a handle to manipulate the crossbar on the letter "H" in the word "Hat." When he turned the crossbar a certain way the batter knew a fast ball was coming, and another way meant a curve was due.

ELMER FOSTER was playing in the outfield for New York one day in 1888, the opposition being furnished by Chicago. The game was nearing its end, and the sun had reached a point where it interfered with Elmer's vision.

A Chicago batter swung furiously, and there was a loud crack as the bat met the ball. As it happened, the batter had topped the ball, and it went bounding to the shortstop, who made an easy play at first.

In the outfield, however, Elmer's ears told him that the ball had been belted high and far; judging from the sound, he even reasoned the ball was coming in his direction. He looked up, and sure enough, there was a speck in the sky, moving in his direction.

The out had already been made and the other players, as well as the fans, were startled at Elmer's behavior. He turned and raced madly toward the fence, occasionally glancing backward and upward, and he had his hands up for a possible catch when he banged up against the fence. The flying dab of something passed over his head and over the fence and vanished. It was a bird.

 LARRY McLEAN, who was a National League catcher years ago, always enjoyed telling the story of how, as a youngster with the St. Louis club, he tricked his own manager in order to get into some ball games.

Day after day Larry found himself on the bench. He couldn't go direct to Manager Charlie Nichols and ask that he be put to work, so he sat and stewed. He had neglected to write to his mother for a couple of weeks so one afternoon while he was sitting on the bench a telegram was delivered to him. His mother simply wanted to know if he was all right.

"Bad news, Larry?" called out one of the other players.

Larry noticed that Manager Nichols was within earshot, so he said in a loud voice:

"No, it's my mother, bless her heart. She just wanted to make sure I wasn't playing ball on Sundays."

"What you going to tell her?" asked his teammate.

"I'm going to tell her not to worry," Larry responded. "Not a chance of it. I can't even get into a game on weekdays, let alone Sundays."

Manager Nichols, of course, heard the remark, and two or three days later Larry was put to work back of the plate.

 MOST BASEBALL FANS spend considerable time wondering what a catcher says to a pitcher during a conference at the mound or what an umpire says to a catcher when they engage in conversation at the plate.

One afternoon in 1897 Baltimore was playing Boston and Wilbert Robinson was catching for Baltimore. Along about the eighth inning the spectators noticed that Robinson and Umpire Tim Hurst were having what appeared to be a violent argument. It went on for a while, died down, and then flared up again. Robinson was hopping mad about something.

Everyone in the stands was talking about it—wondering what the rhubarb was about. So at the end of the game a reporter went to the two men and asked them about it and reconstructed the main part of their conversation at the plate. This is how it went:

HURST: Robbie, what's eating you this afternoon?

ROBINSON: It's these dern shoes I got on, Tim.

HURST: What's the matter with 'em?

ROBINSON: What's the matter with 'em! They're a dad-blame jinx!

HURST: How you figure that?

ROBINSON: Look at the errors I've made already! It's these shoes! I got 'em for security from Billy Earle. Billy borrowed five dollars from me last Tuesday and give me these shoes for security.

HURST: What's that got to do with your errors, Robbie?

ROBINSON: My God, can't you see that? They've jinxed me! Soon as this game's over, I'm giving these shoes back to Billy as fast as I can—five dollars or no five dollars.

HURST: Well, have it your own way.

JOHN PHILIP SOUSA was not only a stanch baseball fan but in 1888 he wrote the score for a comic opera which had baseball as its theme and which was titled *Angela, or The Umpire's Revenge.*

The plot was concerned with the romance of a college baseball pitcher named Eli Yale and a New York lass named Angela.

In the early stages of the thing Eli Yale joined the New York Giants and pitched a game at the Polo Grounds. There was a mean old umpire named Moberly behind the plate, and Eli Yale, at one point, made a polite complaint about the way Moberly was calling them. This enraged Umpire Moberly, and he decided to disrupt Eli's romance with Angela. He did get it all bollixed up for a while, but it came out okay in the end. The musical numbers included "He Stands in the Box with the Ball in His Hand," "The Umpire and the Dude," and "An Umpire I, Who Ne'er Says Die."

There's no way of knowing, but it may well be that this production was the disturbance that brought on the famous Blizzard of '88.

THE GREAT TY COBB was often accused of thinking well of himself. Back in 1911 there was much newspaper talk concerning an "open rebellion" on the part of his Detroit teammates, who said Cobb had a swollen head and domineering attitude.

A couple of years later Cobb was reported as having complained to Manager Hugh Jennings about his assignment to the outfield. Ty wanted a job either pitching or playing an infield position, where he thought he could make a more spectacular showing than in the job of chasing flies.

It came about, then, that on an afternoon in 1913 Manager Jennings gave Cobb his chance and put him on second base for a game between Detroit and Philadelphia. A Detroit sports writer summarized Ty's performance quite masterfully, as follows:

"If the Georgia Gem persists in playing the keystone position, we suggest that he be supplied with the following equipment: one gill net, one dozen sheets of flypaper, one lariat, one pair of shin guards, one setter dog for retrieving purposes, and one map of the infield.

"Eddie Collins, the Athletics' star second baseman, who was nervous at first for fear that a new star might have risen to take his laurels, had hysterics before the afternoon was over, and they had to pound him over the head with a bat before he burst a blood vessel.

"Immediately after the game Collins mailed a dollar to President Navin of the Detroit club, saying that he was ashamed to have all that fun without paying for it.

"Scouts for the leading vaudeville circuits have been summoned by telegraph and will arrive today with contracts that will net Cobb $15,000 a week to play second base on the stage just as he played it in yesterday's game."

Cobb, of course, resumed his career as an outfielder.

WOUNDED PRIDE has often been responsible for weird behavior on the baseball field, a notable case being an incident involving Maurice Powers, M.D.

Maurice Powers was a physician, as indicated, and he was also a catcher for the Philadelphia Athletics in the earliest days of the American League. As a ballplayer he was known as Mike Powers. Some people even called him "Red Cross Mike."

One afternoon in 1906 Jim Dygert, the Philadelphia pitcher, beaned a Boston player named Peterson. Newspaper accounts of the affair said that before the smitten player could fall to the ground, Umpire Silk O'Loughlin had turned toward the crowd and shouted, "Is there a doctor in the stands?"

No doctor immediately appeared, and the fans started yelling for Mike Powers to come to the aid of the fallen man. Mike, however, refused to budge from the Philadelphia bench. A storm of criticism enveloped him as a consequence of his apparent stony indifference. The following day he defended his conduct in this way:

"My professional dignity was outraged. Silk howled for a grandstand doctor before Peterson hit the ground, and Silk knew well enough that I was on the bench. Had he asked, 'Is there a doctor on the bench?' I would have responded at once, but they wanted a grandstand doctor and had to wait for one.

"The medical gentleman who did appear later is a friend of mine. As he passed the bench he asked me to join him in consultation over the beaned player, but I declined. My professional dignity would not permit me even to consult in a case where I had been thrown down in the first place."

 IN 1893, the year that he joined Chicago as a pitcher, Clark Griffith had finished out the season when a man from California approached him.

"Griff," he said, "I have a proposition to make to you, involving a chance for you to pick up a nice piece of change."

The proposition concerned two neighboring towns in California, each of which had a strong amateur baseball team. The two teams were soon to meet for the amateur championship of California. Griffith's visitor was representing one of these teams.

He wanted the Chicago pitcher to travel out to California and, under an assumed name, do the hurling for the club he represented. After terms were agreed upon the emissary then asked Griffith to engage the services of several other National League players to be used as ringers.

Griffith and four or five other big-league players proceeded to the coast town, put on some shabby uniforms, took a roundabout course to reach the ball park, and on arrival went onto the field to limber up. A huge crowd was on hand, and there was much betting on the game. Griffith and his fellow ringers were getting ready to pool their cash resources and get a wager down on their team, when the opposing club arrived on the diamond.

"When they came into view," Griffith recalled years later, "the first man I saw was Jerry Denny, who played infield for New York. Behind him was Big Bill Brown, the Giants catcher. Then I saw Fred Carroll, and after him came several other top professionals. In fact the other team had more and better ringers than we had. Naturally we forgot about making any bets."

All of the ringers for each team played the entire game, and not once did one of them give an indication that he recognized the others, lest the whole plot explode and the pay be withheld. The game was a close one, but Griffith's side won it, to become the amateur champions of California.

 THE ELKS of Zanesville, Ohio, were not only benevolent and protective back in 1909 but they were fairly bursting with brotherly love.

Among their members was a baseball pitcher named Kenworthy, who played with the Zanesville team.

In the winter of that year Kenworthy was drafted by the Columbus club of the American Association. This came as a severe blow to the Zanesville Elks. They couldn't bear the thought of losing such a fine fellow, so they called an emergency meeting and raised a purse of $600. They took this money to the management of the local baseball team together with a request that it be used to buy Kenworthy back from Columbus. The transaction was accomplished without difficulty.

It was a pretty gesture, containing elements of love and loyalty and sacrifice; yet, as always, there were people who gossiped and sneered about it. Behind their hands they said that there was a good enough reason why the Elks wanted Kenworthy to stay in Zanesville. Didn't he play poker every Saturday night at the clubrooms? And wasn't he the world's worst poker player? And didn't he usually lose his pay check to the other Elks?

A FRIEND of the workingman (baseball-playing division) made a profound proposal back in 1894 in an essay written for the Detroit *Journal*, under which ballplayers would no longer have to suffer under an economic system by which they got regular pay. The Detroit thinker recommended that they be paid on a piecework basis.

He was inspired by the fact that in a single day of that 1894 season three Western League teams produced an over-all total of one hundred and nine runs.

"It is not fair," said the essayist, "to work men as hard as the players did that day. It would be more desirable all around if the men were paid by what they do rather than so much a week or a month."

He then proposed the following piecework scale:

Runs	50 cents each
Put-outs	40 cents each
Assists	30 cents each
Singles	10 cents each
Two-base hits	20 cents each
Triples	30 cents each
Home runs	40 cents each
Sacrifice hits	05 cents each
Stolen bases	05 cents each

He did not make it quite clear just how much a home-run hitter would get—presumably forty cents for the homer and another fifty cents for scoring. Errors, he suggested, would be charged against the player on a sliding scale, and there would be a special scale for pitchers.

The authors of this book hereby grant permission to one sports writer in each city to employ this system in reporting one game during the current season. Let's not overdo it, men.

 IN RECENT TIMES the people of St. Louis have occasionally been charged with apathy when it comes to baseball. There was a time, however, when St. Louis was regarded as the most enthusiastic baseball city in the nation.

In the 1880s the Browns were under the ownership of Chris Von der Ahe and managed by Charlie Comiskey. This team won four successive pennants, and the people of St. Louis fairly worshiped the organization as well as its individual members.

The adulation bestowed upon the Browns reached a climax, perhaps, when the management of the Missouri Pacific Railroad announced in 1888 that it was naming four stations on its line after star performers on the team. Those so honored were Foutz, Latham, Bushong, and Comiskey. Examination of present-day maps shows that these towns still exist.

 SOME PEOPLE still contend that Rube Waddell was the greatest pitcher ever to hold a ball in his hand. It is certain that the Rube ranks among the most colorful ballplayers in the history of the game. He was in and out of scrapes more often than he was in and out of ball games, and newspapermen of his day were kept busy recording his extramural shenanigans with whisky and women.

Such was the Rube's greatness on the mound, however, that men quarreled for years over the question of who "discovered" him.

Old newspaper files, while not exactly settling the argument, tell a fairly straight story, and an amusing one, of the Rube's beginnings in baseball.

As a grown boy he worked on his father's farm just outside the town of Butler in Pennsylvania.

"It was while he was tilling the soil," says one account, "that he earned the sobriquet of 'Rube,' by which he later was to be known wherever baseball was played. And those who applied the name to him certainly made no mistake, for he certainly looked the part. Guiding the plow and handling other agricultural implements swelled the muscles of the farm boy's arms to the size and hardness of pig-iron ingots. He could throw a stone out of sight with either hand. It was an easy matter for him, so true was his aim, to bring down a bird on the wing with a piece of rock picked up from the ground."

Young Waddell began pitching for the amateur team in Butler, but after a while he was compelled to quit because he was too good. Teams from other villages complained that they could not hit the ball at all when he was pitching, and soon they were refusing to play Butler with Rube in the line-up. Scouts from larger towns approached him, but he was bashful, afraid to travel farther than a few miles from the farm, and he turned them all down.

Then one day a traveling minstrel troupe came to Butler. Rube took in the street parade and the show and got the fever—this was the thing he wanted to do. He ran away from home and joined the show.

Some weeks later the minstrel troupe marched into the town of DuBois, and there in all his glory was young Rube Waddell leading the parade, wearing a multicolored uniform with epaulets and spangles, an elegant, if somewhat ratty, shako on his head, and swinging a drum major's baton with his pitching hand.

It happened that the show arrived on a day when a spirited ball game was to be played between DuBois and Punxsutawney. It also happened that a DuBois hotel proprietor named Henry J. Spuhler recognized the big, ungainly drum major as the farm boy who pitched so well for Butler that he was barred from the game.

A big delegation of Punxsutawney citizens swarmed through the streets of DuBois, waving fistfuls of currency, offering to

bet it all on their team. But there were few takers. DuBois had a good ball team but was weak in one department—pitching.

When the minstrel parade was over, Spuhler, the hotel man, quietly made his way to the town's opera house and confronted Rube Waddell. He made him an offer, but the Rube would hear nothing of it—he didn't wanna play no dad-burn baseball no more; he liked this here show business. Spuhler didn't give up, however, and argued on and finally offered Rube the enormous sum of twenty dollars if he would pitch for DuBois. Now Rube was tempted and began considering the proposition and finally he said he'd do it "with a per-vide." He'd pitch, he said, "per-vided" he could do it wearing his spangled uniform and his tall fur hat.

That, then, was the way he appeared on the mound in the first game he ever pitched for pay. The Punxsutawney partisans laughed fit to kill at the beginning and splashed more money around, and now they were finding takers.

The splendidly caparisoned yokel went to work, and when it was over the score book showed that he had struck out nineteen men and that not a single batter had been able to hit the ball out of the infield. The entire town of DuBois went wild over him, and the celebration lasted all night, with the hero in the middle of it. When the minstrel show moved on, Rube was not with it. He stayed behind and pitched some more for DuBois, and soon his fame was spreading and the scouts from the bigger towns were seeking him out. He moved along to better teams in Pennsylvania and then to Louisville, where he began his major-league career—with a bottle in each hand.

 BASEBALL PLAYERS should be careful when they dally with the arts—they might find themselves trapped.

In 1908 the St. Louis Browns had a pitcher named Happy Howell. He was a first-rate pitcher for six or seven innings and then he usually ran into trouble. "I can go just about six innings," he explained, "and then I get trouble with my stomach and blow up."

His stomach trouble was widely discussed at the time, and then one day somebody told him that he needed special exercises aimed at strengthening his abdominal muscles.

"Take up singing," said his advisor, "because that's the best way to strengthen those muscles. Do a lot of singing, and before long your stomach trouble will be over."

So Happy Howell started singing. And pretty soon he found himself liking singing better than he liked baseball. And then— he simply announced that he was abandoning baseball because he wanted to try for a career in grand opera. So far as can be learned at this late date he never made it.

TIM HURST, the colorful umpire of yesteryear, was a man who liked the bright lights of Broadway. Whenever he was assigned to umpire a series in Philadelphia he usually made a practice of riding up to New York after a game, staying all night in Manhattan, and returning the next morning.

On those days when he was planning his New York trip Tim had a habit of pulling out his watch and looking at it during the late stages of the game in Philadelphia. Whenever possible he tried to catch the train which left North Philadelphia at five-fifteen.

One afternoon when Tim was worrying his watch the Athletics went into the eighth inning leading St. Louis by eleven runs. It had been a slow game, and Umpire Hurst was fretting more than usual over the chance that he'd miss that train.

Pitching for St. Louis was Jack Powell, who knew about Tim and the five-fifteen. Pitcher Powell reflected on the fact that his team was hopelessly behind and decided to have some fun. He began pitching "wild" deliberately. He walked batters and threw the ball over the catcher's head. He pretended that he was unable to catch signals, delaying things even more, much to the discomfiture of Umpire Hurst.

Then Hurst began to suspect that Powell was deliberately trying to slow up the game and make him miss his train.

"Come on," he yelled out to the pitcher, "get that ball acrost!"

Powell stuck his tongue out at the umpire. More words were exchanged, and Powell gave himself away. Now Tim Hurst *knew* that Powell was trying to make him miss that train.

In the ninth inning Powell continued his wildness—got worse, if anything. But he pitched only nine balls. No matter where they went—five feet wide of the plate, six feet above the catcher's head—Tim Hurst called every one of them a strike. Nine pitched balls, nine strikes, three outs, and Tim caught the five-fifteen.

THE FIRST World Series was played in 1903, with the Boston Americans beating the Pittsburgh Nationals five games to three. One of the odd facts about this first series concerns the player pools. The Red Sox won, and each member of the team got $1,182. The Pirates lost, and each man got $1,316. The explanation lies in the fact that Barney Dreyfuss, the Pittsburgh owner, tossed the club's share into the players' pool while Henry Killilea, owner of the Red Sox, chose to keep his $6,699.56.

There was no World Series the following year. The Boston Red Sox again won the American League pennant, while the New York Giants took the National League championship. The Red Sox challenged the Giants, but John T. Brush, president of the New York club, wanted no part of a post-season series. He issued a statement which said:

"There is nothing in the constitution or playing rules of the National League which requires its victorious club to submit its championship honors to a contest with a victorious club in a minor league.

"Neither the players nor the manager of the Giants nor myself desires any greater glory than to win the pennant in the National League. That is the greatest honor that can be obtained in baseball."

Within a very few years the boys from the "minor league" were fairly consistently beating the brains out of the New York Giants whenever the Giants managed to get into a World Series.

THERE'S a commonplace saying in baseball that nobody loves a base hit so dearly as a pitcher. This axiom applied, certainly, in the case of James Galvin, who was as famous a half century ago as a man could ever want to be. Jim Galvin was famous, however, as a pitcher and not as a hitter. He was, in fact, popularly regarded as the worst hitter who ever held a bat in his hand. It was natural, therefore, that his heart's desire was to get a base hit.

One afternoon Jim came to the plate with two men out and the bases loaded. Everybody in the park, including Jim himself, figured him for an easy out. The opposing pitcher wound up and let one come. Jim closed his eyes and swung with all his might. Wham! The ball took off nobly, headed for the depths of center field, and Jim headed for first as hard as he could go. It looked like a sure triple that would clean the bases—maybe even a home run. Lord, but he felt good! He rounded first and galloped toward second, raising his head to have a look at center field and find out what was going on in those parts. What he saw all but unhinged his mind: the center fielder leaped high in the air and speared the ball in a spectacular one-handed catch.

Jim Galvin stopped running for only a brief moment. A fury possessed him now, and when he resumed running he was no longer on the base paths—he was headed straight for center field, and there was murder in his heart. Even from a distance the center fielder saw that Galvin meant him no good; he turned and scampered to the fence and, arriving there, climbed quickly to the top of it. In a moment Galvin was below him, and it looked as if he were going to climb after the inconsiderate outfielder. He decided against it, however, and just stood below his man. Then he talked—talked in an ungentle tone, talked unendingly—and the language he used, they say, took three coats of paint off the fence and loosened knots in the boards for a distance of forty feet.

A CLERGYMAN in Ashland, Pennsylvania, wrestled with his conscience for a while in 1907 and then issued the following statement:

"Sunday baseball is deplorably wrong in principle. But it must be admitted that this year the Sunday games have broken up the Sunday beer picnics. The breaking up of those picnics has materially lessened the number of crimes for the September Criminal Court. Besides this, it must be recognized that young people can attend ball games on Sunday afternoon and still be able to attend church services in the evening with a clear mind, if not a clear conscience. But those who are out on drunken carousals are totally unfit for attendance at public worship. If it comes to a choice of the two evils, baseball is certainly the lesser."

 THERE WAS a time in the early days of baseball when people who lived near the railroad tracks in the rural areas of the nation could tell when a passing train was carrying a touring ball club. If the side of the train bore a resemblance to a Monday-morning wash line, that meant that a baseball team was on board.

In those days the ordinary ball park had no dressing rooms for the players of visiting clubs, and they were required to go from the park to their hotels before changing clothes. Often when time was short they went straight to their train in their uniforms.

Facilities for cleaning and laundering uniforms also were scarce in those times, so that it became a custom among players, once they were aboard a train, to take care of their own playing outfits. Each player carried his equipment in a "uniform roll," and at the start of a train trip he would unfurl it and shake out the various garments, which usually were soaked with perspira-

236

tion and saturated with dirt. He would then raise the train window and hang his shirt and trousers and socks outside in the rushing air, lowering the sash to secure each article of apparel. It didn't take many miles to dry out the uniform and whip a good part of the dust out of it.

THERE IS EVIDENCE that John L. Sullivan was quite a baseball player before he took up prize fighting. His boyhood home was near the South End ball park in Boston, and he was, at one time, player-manager of an independent team which toured New England.

After Sullivan became heavyweight champion of the world he continued to be an enthusiastic baseball fan, attending major-league games regularly. And when his public clamored for him to appear on the field and show his muscles, John L. had a little stunt for their edification. He'd stand on home plate and let the fielders throw balls at his chest as hard as they could.

THE FIRST no-hit game on record (says our research department) was slung at New Haven, Connecticut, by a young man named Joseph Mc-Elroy Mann, pitching for Princeton University against Yale. The date: May 29, 1875.

Inasmuch as there had been nothing in the nature of a no-hitter up to then, the newspaper took little cognizance of the Mann performance—please remember that the man who ate that first oyster didn't get his name in the papers. A complete report of that New Haven game, as it appeared in the New York *Mercury*, occupied one paragraph, which follows:

> The game between the Princeton and Yale clubs in New Haven yesterday was one of the finest of the season. Mr. Mann's pitching for the Princeton nine was so effective that the Yales did not make a single base hit. The Princetons won by a score of 8 to 0. Woods and Duffield of the Princetons particularly distinguished themselves, the latter taking several beautiful flies after hard runs.

 TUG ARUNDEL, a catcher for Washington in the 1890s, never lived down the Piggy Ward incident.

Washington and Baltimore were playing one afternoon, and the Baltimore boys came to bat in the last of the ninth, trailing by three runs.

Tug Arundel was working behind the plate. Baltimore got the bases filled, with two men out, when Piggy Ward came to bat. This Piggy Ward had a tongue like a rattail file, and he had been using it all afternoon on Tug, abusing the Washington catcher unmercifully.

Now, at this critical moment, Piggy stood at the plate and out of the corner of his mouth resumed his caustic commentary on Tug's looks, talents, ancestors, and so forth.

Piggy let two pitches get past him, and both were strikes.

"Furthermore," he growled at the catcher, "you're so clumsy you couldn't put the tag on a half-dead hound dog."

"Yeh?" growled Tug. "You wait'll the next time I get a chance to put the tag on you. I'll bust yer goddamn ribs!"

Just then the pitch came in, and the umpire called it strike three, and Tug Arundel dropped it. That gave Piggy an opportunity to run down to first. Tug had plenty of time to make the throw and end the game and the inning, but he wanted to bust some ribs, so instead of throwing to first, he picked up the ball and started chasing Piggy. He chased him to first and beyond and kept after him along the route to second, and Piggy was still out ahead of him as they went down to third, and on they came—in to home plate, and Piggy scored before the big catcher could overtake him. The three other runners, of course, scored ahead of Piggy, giving the contest to Baltimore. In his wholesome fury Tug Arundel had forgotten all about those other runners.

BASEBALL was affected, of course, by the high feeling that accompanied the War Between the States. In June of 1863 the New York *Mercury* reported the following:

> The moment the Excelsiors received satisfactory assurance that Pearsall of their club had gone over

to the Rebels, he was at once expelled from the club.

This is an example that other
clubs should follow that have the
names of similar black sheep on their
books. A Northern man that would
become a traitor to his flag to serve a
slave oligarchy is beneath contempt.
The least to be done is to erase the
name of such a fellow from the
books of any loyal association he may
have belonged to, and the club that
does not do it should be expelled
from the National Association.

A MAJOR LEAGUER named Bob Unglaub listened to all the talk back in 1907 about the need
for more hitting in baseball as a means of increasing
public interest in the game. Mr. Unglaub then came up with
an idea.

He suggested that a white line in the form of an arc be
drawn on the field, starting at the foul lines, eighty yards from
home plate so that the distance from the plate to any point on
the arc would be eighty yards. Outfielders, under the Unglaub
plan, would be required to play within that line until the bat
hit the ball. Only then could a fielder start running. In other
words, outfielders would be forbidden under this scheme from
ever "playing deep" for heavy hitters. The Unglaub proposal
evoked much discussion, but nothing, of course, ever came
of it.

ARTHUR RAYMOND, the great pitcher for the New York Giants back in the early years of the century, was called "Bugs" for the reason that he was somewhat bugs. His eccentricities were many and varied, and he loved to look upon the wine when it was just any old color at all. It is recorded that one afternoon when he was sent down to the bull pen with instructions to get himself warmed up, he slipped away, went to a saloon across the street from the park, and traded the ball for a couple of king-size snorts.

In 1910 a sports writer reported that Bugs was the only ballplayer in the country with a perpetual guardian, in the person of Dick Fuller, a former Pinkerton detective.

"Fuller," the writer said, "travels constantly with Raymond, accompanying him to and from the ball park, sharing hotel rooms with him, and keeping an eagle's watch upon his actions. Fuller carries the purse and buys Bugs all the lemonade he wishes and stops there. The guardian is a big chap, going over two hundred pounds, and is a physical match for Raymond."

 THE SPIKES which adorn a baseball player's shoes have been put to many wicked uses, yet there is one case in which they may have saved a man's life.

Jack Lively, playing with the Oakland club in 1910, went shopping one day in San Francisco. He bought a pair of baseball shoes and then went into a bank to cash a check for a hundred dollars. When he came out he soon discovered that three tough-looking men were following him. He was in a mean part of the city and he was worried. He stepped along briskly until he came to a cheap hotel. There he decided to hire a room and get in it and thus escape his pursuers.

Soon after entering the room, he heard stealthy footsteps outside the door. Then he heard men whispering, and after that the sound of a key in the lock.

Jack quickly unwrapped his new shoes, with the thought of using them as weapons. Then he had an idea. He took a shoe in each hand and clicked the metal spikes together to make a sound like the cocking of a revolver.

"The first so-and-so that sticks his head through that door gets it shot off!" he yelled.

All he heard after that was the sound of retreat, and he saw no more of the thugs.

 OUR WORD "mascot" derives from the French and in France means "a little sorcerer or magician." Mascots in our country usually are associated with athletic organizations and are either small boys or animals. In the game of baseball the mascot has generally been utilitarian— it's all right to have him around for good luck, but the little twerp oughta do some work too. Hence the combination bat boy and mascot—a goal to which many an American boy has set his dreamy eyes.

Many have made it, but none ever tried to do so well at it as the lad who handled the bats and the juvenile sorcery for the Philadelphia Athletics in 1912. In March of that year the team went down to Baltimore for a pre-season game. In those days individual lockers were rare, so each of the Philadelphia players before taking the field wrapped his cash and other valuables in a handkerchief, and these little bundles were placed in a satchel which was kept near the bench.

Along about the fifth inning of that game someone noticed that the satchel was missing. Then someone else noticed that the team's little sorcerer or magician, age fourteen, also had disappeared.

A quick checkup showed that the missing bag contained upward of twenty-five hundred dollars in valuables and money, and the alarm was sounded for the mascot.

Police found him the same day and recovered the loot. The boy had let flaming ambition get the better of his good sense. He said he took the money so he could finance the organization of a team of boys, with himself as manager. "I figured," he said, "I would grow up to be a fine manager like Connie Mack."